More praise for Peter J. Harris' *Bless the Ashes*

"In *Bless the Ashes,* we are taken to the place where personal and public space ⌐⌐ ⌐ge. These writings of healing honor the male essence with sensuality ⌐⌐ e. Blessed by the Orishas, this ofrenda, a word shrine sung ⌐⌐ ⌐f Peter J. Harris, is unafraid, revolutionary in sp⌐⌐⌐

—Gloria Enedina Alvarez, author of *La Excusa/Ti*

"It takes patience to fold a crane and even m⌐ piness. Harris folds words into fitful cranes t⌐ ⌐ackled edges of juke joints, sinking fields of cement f⌐ ⌐⌐ ⌐o the next. And as they land, they unfold into poems: simultaneousl⌐ ⌐⌐ and ancient; bed rock and vessel; hollow gogo drum and full-bodied bass; molten desire and dawn of morning after. These poems are legacy and lifeline as only a luminary such as Harris can offer up."

—Ariel Robello, author of *My Sweet Unconditional*

" 'Poetry is nothing but healthy speech,' Thoreau claimed, and Peter Harris's poetry gives us the spoken voice at its most vital and robust, intensified and lyricized, but always speaking credible human speech, from the heart, from the soul, from a mind honed to a kind of holy precision. 'First thing out my mouth you know I believe in praise,' Harris writes, and there's nothing faint about his praising. His language is fierce and fluid, full of dash and fire and flash and rigor, sensual and ethical in the same breath, a kind of 'liquid scripture,' as he says, calling for 'less shock and more awe;' Ginsbergian in its condemnation of the 'blood-lust corroding a nation's central nervous system;' insisting, in an incantatory poem to his lost/never lost mother, June—or is it the voice of the mother we hear, reminding him, reminding all of us? – that 'every good that's ever died is alive.' These poems are incantatory and incendiary. They will set your heart on fire. They will make you want to get up and dance in your most human skin. They are some of the most necessary poems I have ever known."

—Cecilia Woloch, author of *Carpathia, Tsigan: The Gypsy Poem*

"Peter Harris is the master of the language of love in poetry. For years now, he has been able to express the beauty of the human spirit like few writers, effortlessly, and as if he was talking to you on your front porch or on a slow bus ride across town. This astonishing volume of verse is more of the gifts he has always given: soulful and precious words and phrasings, honest, proud, and always surprising, improvising infinitely, elevating black word to its rightful place in our world."

—Brian Gilmore, author of *Jungle Nights* and *Soda Fountain Rags: Poem for Duke Ellington*
and *elvis presley is alive and well and living in harlem*

"Peter Harris constantly reminds us that LOVE is the first four-letter word and that love's origin, like the instigation of all action and interaction, is hidden deep in the cellular structure of our very humanity and at the same time manifest daily for all to see, hear, feel, taste and sense. His poetry creates the double perception of light and elevation that allows the other become witness, congregant, participant, and heroically choose a real path."

—K. Curtis Lyle, author of *Electric Church*

"Peter J. Harris is a self-proclaimed risk taker who has a strong sense of history and its rivals. He is not afraid to ask 'whose child am I?'; is not afraid to confront, confuse, stun and comfort. He knows he is 'complete' and 'one atom away from joy.' Read his work— that atom will be left in his dust."

—Lynne Thompson, author of *Start with a Small Guitar* and *Beg No Pardon*

"From the first poignant introductory poem, 'I Know I Ain't Hip No More,' to the last poem … *Bless the Ashes* shows how the author has come full circle in his life, within his art, and towards a complete acceptance of himself as a man who loves his community and humanity with his eyes open wide—and nothing is off limits here. The first poem is a bold entrenchment that hip hop's unfortunate transformation from conscious constructive language to oppressive negative imagery has alienated not only Harris' generation, but any poet or artist with something meaningful to contribute: 'I make eye contact with babies on the street/to catch my stares they twist in their parents' arms/ignore shouts against talking to strangers…I might as well be wearing red socks & highwaters… if microwave cool is the style/if the password is knee-jerk ideology/if sweet talking power brokers gets me over/I know I ain't hip no more.'

"In the sensual poems as well as the poems full of mirth, and even in poems about his mother, Peter's narrative shows fearlessness. We see the author's love and respect of Stevie Wonder and Marvin Gaye, as well as an unabashed love of black men without stigma. The poems show a candor and opulence reminiscent of an ancient generation of wordsmiths whose job and purpose was to provide foundational self-knowledge and awareness, while charging the next generation with a mission—speak truth; Speak true. Yet there are also personal and political poems such as 'Come Sunday' that wrestle with demons, moments that Harris considers his and society's shortcomings, questions his worth measured against failure and possibly society's failure to fulfill him:

> whose child am I?
> Black vegetarian with simple hungers hope of a refugee
> charmed by circle & sine waves
> in greeting or touch or instrument
> or greeting in the touch of hand on a cello or kora
> sweeping failure into the song circling failure
> centrifuge spinning…

"Along with the 'spinning,' there is also a pervasive motif of 'baptism' that calls us to wash things clean. To be ready at any and every moment, to renew and redo a life, a mistake, a misspoken word or deed: Harris allows us the needed room to forgive ourselves, and to remember that, much like James Baldwin contended in one interview, 'our humanity is more important that any race, creed or religion.'

"Particularly in the poem, 'Bless the Ashes,' for his mother, we see the poet's earnest struggle and wrangling with finding love in mourning: *I call on my June/*January mother with summer name/I call on her New York voice freed from tracheotomy tube/to mash lumps of bad memories until I'm gravy again/*I call on my June//* to help me bless the ashes of my ripening/as I flower finally in the compost of her death & my heartbreaks.'

Bless the Ashes is a *tour de force* collection of poems that simmers in your lap. It vibrates with the pulse of the seeker, with Harris' questions upon questions to get to the meat of the thing, and ultimately, leaves the reader wanting to be a part of something whole and righteous. Something at once old and new. Something pure and simple, like a baby's laughter or smile, which Harris references often. These poems make a poet want to write. The poems make you want to spit fire. Make you want to cry and laugh at the same time. And if mere words can evoke such a feeling, proving that language is both wet kiss love, and penetrating weapon, then the poet has done his job. Good on you, Peter J. Harris, good on you."

— Shonda Buchanan, MFA, Assistant Professor of Creative Writing and English,
  Hampton University; author of *Who's Afraid of Black Indians?*

"Fifteen minutes or ten, prayer or moan, the timing of this work is not random. Sacred never is. Through the ceremony of word-water and muse, Peter J. Harris invites us to own that we be 'Complete Already' and I believe him."

—V.Kali, Anansi Writer's Workshop Coordinator, The World Stage, Los Angeles

Bless
the Ashes

*Door of No Return — portal through which Africans were forced
during the Atlantic Triangle Trade.*

Bless the ashes

POEMS

Peter J. Harris

TIA CHUCHA PRESS

ISBN 978-1-882688-49-4

Book Design: Jane Brunette
Back cover author photo: Adenike A. Harris

Published by:
Tia Chucha Press
A Project of Tia Chucha's Centro Cultural, Inc.
PO Box 328
San Fernando, CA 91341
www.tiachucha.org

Distributed by:
Northwestern University Press
Chicago Distribution Center
11030 South Langley Avenue
Chicago IL 60628

Tia Chucha's Centro Cultural & Bookstore is a 501 (c) 3 nonprofit corporation funded in part over
the years by the National Endowment for the Arts, California Arts Council, Los Angeles County Arts
Commission, Los Angeles Department of Cultural Affairs, The California Community Foundation,
the Annenberg Foundation, the Weingart Foundation, the Lia Fund, National Association of Latino
Arts and Culture, Ford Foundation, MetLife, Southwest Airlines, the Andy Warhol Foundation for
the Visual Arts, the Thrill Hill Foundation, the Middleton Foundation, Center for Cultural Innova-
tion, John Irvine Foundation, Not Just Us Foundation, the Attias Family Foundation, and the Gua-
camole Fund, among others. Donations have also come from Bruce Springsteen, John Densmore of
The Doors, Jackson Browne, Lou Adler, Richard Foos, Gary Stewart, Charles Wright, Adrienne Rich,
Tom Hayden, Dave Marsh, Jack Kornfield, Jesus Trevino, David Sandoval, Denise Chávez and John
Randall of the Border Book Festival, Luis & Trini Rodríguez, and others.

Contents

HAUNTED LOVERS

WATER ON IT

COMPLETE ALREADY

Preface

Yes: Peter J. Harris
and the Wonderment of Words

THOSE WHO WRITE and/or study poetry understand the many obstacles in reaching a level of proficiency, readability, skillfulness, competence, connectedness, love of language, and process that good poetry requires. Many poets pursue poetry as a life's work after reading and scrutinizing the best poets of their tradition. For me, I grew into poetry with the best of our tradition through writers like James Weldon Johnson, Paul Laurence Dunbar, Claude McKay, Jean Toomer, Sterling A. Brown, Langston Hughes, Gwendolyn Brooks, Melvin B. Tolson, Margaret Walker, Amiri Baraka, Margaret Danner, Dudley Randall, Mari Evans and Robert Hayden to name a few. Upon reading Peter J. Harris's current collection, "Bless the Ashes," it becomes obvious that many, if not all, of the same poets and more have also influenced him. He, in this singular book, has navigated his language and ideas like a seasoned musician soloing after receiving private lessons from John Coltrane and Nina Simone.

My engagement with this poet is not accidental. After over four decades of writing, editing, publishing, and teaching, I have had ample opportunity to interact with and read literally thousands of poets and every once in a Black moon I would come across a poem by Peter Harris. I remember his earlier work because of his unique ability to fuse the aesthetic with the political in a form that was not oppressive, trite or limiting. As a young poet, as all of us were, he was searching for his language. In *Bless the Ashes*, he has found it: concentrated, energized, and committed. His ideas are fresh, illuminating, and embracing. He is a poet who challenges us. He gives us history as art, confirming that there is little connectedness in poetry without truth, self-giving, and culture. However, there is something grander in his work, not tangential to the circle but in it, a healing substance that demands that we think, smile and act. This is healthy poetry with a conscience and a smile, revealing rooted introspection and quiet love.

In *Bless the Ashes*, Peter Harris's command of first lines pushes us forward into each poem. Read these engaging and inviting lines: "I make eye contact with babies on the street," or "wake up a failure," or "January mother with summer name," or "lay deep in the hidden pockets," or "put down your gun/pick up your baby," and "her face shaped from stubborn cell division plaits corn-rowed from double-dutch strands." These randomly chosen quotes from this powerful collection provide human eye assurance of the magical unfolding of what is to come.

Peter Harris gives us history as art, as poetry, as a complete narrative of his poetic interaction with many worlds; his and others all subjective, material and that which can't be easily observed by eyes wide open. He is not an easy poet, however, he is peacefully accessible to those who are willing to give him a careful read. His humanity is large and uncompromising, but also he is open to misreading if one doesn't take time to embrace his geography and architecture. "Peter, you ain't Black, you vegetarian!" not on the main streets of the Black community or most other communities. The poet Adrienne Rich has written that, "critical discourse about poetry has said little about conditions of our material existence, past and present." Reading *Bless the Ashes* supplies keys for both doors and other worlds.

One of his poems, specifically the title of the poem "Sacred Places Surrender to the Word," delineates the content and meaning of this entire collection. His references—from Donny Hathaway to Malcolm X, from Aretha to Marley—all contribute to the big picture, an outer space photograph of earth. One of my favorite poems among many is "Grooved Pavement Ahead," where he "unveils synergy of laughter," a forerunner to an "empathy of geopolitical emotions / refuses assigned role as local color to the police state." He writes:

> I have never banned a people's language,
> snatched children from their cultures' briar patch
> slandered a maroon
> posse-pounded after a family running into independence
> sewn passbooks into the seams of innocent citizens
> fractured justice in Black codes fugitive slave law patriot acts

Toni Morrison, in her Nobel Lecture in Literature, writes: "The systematic looting of language can be recognized by the tendency of its users to forgo its nuanced, complex, mid-wifery properties, replacing them with menace and subjugation. Oppressive language does more than represent violence; it is violence; does more than represents the limits of knowledge; it limits knowledge."

I maintain that Peter J. Harris, in this work, gives and expands knowledge, poetically fights and negates violence, and strategically suggests correctives that only art is capable of achieving. He gives and expands knowledge with poems that are anti-racist, pro-women and children, offering us as original quilt of come on in, but you have to use your mind.

Whether writing carefully in free verse, prose poetry, multi-stanza un-rhymed lines, or as a musician with words, Peter Harris constantly surrounds us with his superior ability to communicate his ideas into poetic form, always "finding haven in the fusion of still movement." Poet as lover, and like most artists, shares intimate moments in "1,000 O' Clock" and writes of his memorable "aftershock" in "Another Sunken Treasure" where he and his mate slept "beneath... satisfied earth." His use of repetition and harmony, his distinction between personal and public voices, all culminate into a Black laden inclusive collage. Gwendolyn Brooks in *Primer For Blacks* writes that "we still need the essential Black statement of defense and definition ... in spite of all the disappointment and disillusionment and befuddlement there, I go on believing that the Weak among us will, finally, perceive the impressiveness of our numbers, perceive the quality and legitimacy of our essence, and take sufficient, indicated steps toward definition, clarification."

Bless the Ashes, a book of clarification and validation, represents "sufficient, indicated steps." Mr. Harris' many seasons of life are on selective display as well as his community, which is constantly written off and imprisoned—literally and figuratively—but never defeated. His essential message remains, "don't be foiled or fooled by the zip code / the ocean is ours / the mountain is ours / the river is ours / the forest is ours / the sky is ours / anything less no / to anything less no / to anything less / their horizons & freedom & justice / & peace & humanity / day in & day out day in & day out..." Yet, none of my observations on the extraordinary dynamism, energy and insight, in this collection can match the poet's own reflection on his life:

> there are Black men in our lives
> always
> yes, Black men
> in our lives
> there's always a Black man in our lives
> always
> in our lives
> alive alive alive *well*

I say amen, and as Sonia Sanchez would say, awomen.

—*Haki R. Madhubuti*
Founder and publisher of Third World Press;
author of *Honoring Genius: Gwendolyn Brooks
The Narrative of Craft, Art, Kindness and Justice*

I KNOW I AIN'T HIP NO MORE

I make eye contact with babies on the street
to catch my stares they twist in their parents' arms
ignore shouts against talking to strangers

today
I beam the babies' priorities into my neighborhood
sprinkle talcum powder between warring adults
breathe heated massage oil into frozen egos

tonight
I sneak along deserted streets in your town
paste clown faces over Dewar's Profiles
spray paint Benson & Hedges with infant smiles

I know I ain't hip no more
I sculpt wind in a toddler's laugh
I cuddle trends that could answer Marvin Gaye's cry
                              (save the babies/save the children)

I might as well be wearing red socks & highwaters
to a late 70s GoGo in Southeast D.C.
or wearing lemon double knit Sands-a-Belts
& clapping despite Sandman's pan at the Apollo

clomping in two-tone platform shoes
& escorting a Valley Girl to a house party
or shading my eyes with a Gangsterlean widebrim
& pumping up the volume on the *Muzak* Top 10

if microwave cool is the style
if the password is knee-jerk ideology
if sweet talking power brokers gets me over

I know I ain't hip no more
I know I ain't hip no more

TRUE RISK pivots on the smallest ball bearing. Opens a 3rd Eye on any Ill Hierarchy. It's deeply personal and humbling. Haunts what seem to be almost pedestrian crossroads and thresholds. Risk is never generic. Plunging into integrity demanded in real time is riskiest: Can I say no when yes is easier? Will I disagree when nodding OK keeps the peace? Will I risk sounding defensive in order to defend myself, or my principles? In my poems, I don't consider risky anything technical. I respect traditional forms. Mostly, I'm drawn into structure by each poem's music. No theme is taboo. Risk, for me, is fighting self-censorship. Peeping and avoiding tendencies. Tapping my ethical voice. Converting rage. Cultivating virtuosity. Salvaging my subtlety. Trusting the immaterial. Honoring innocence. Working the inspirational without being naive. I don't court risk. I'm inevitably subject to its constant velocity.

- PETER J. HARRIS TO KHADIJAH QUEEN

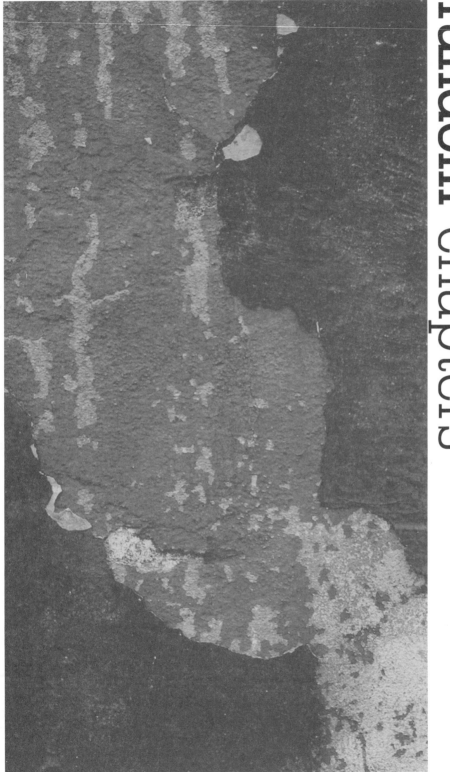

random chapters

First Thing Out My Mouth

too much out the mouth *heavyscented* with photocopied PR
a radar spoof   spit mirror   dazed faces revolving
        make somebody wheeze
        when they should breathe deep as a yoga teacher
        in dreads & cotton drawstring consultation
it's too easy to come with
stale anger   stylish breakdown   or foggy know-it-all
hip only with downloaded sound of the day mashed between gritted teeth
jaws too locked to exhale the citrus inside
        first thing out my mouth you know I believe in praise
        call a man brother   call a woman sister
        split a compliment to the core so fast
        fruit spill out the sides of my love

speaking for my own self
without even a *New Jack* interlocutor
seem like too much out the mouth marinated in ammonia
leaping synaptic gap or soaking files of government
spoke with no Home Training   no regard for law
no regard for past or tomorrow
        first thing out my mouth you know I
        want a boy become a man   want a girl become a woman
        to help me face down bureaucrats
        waving leather bound official legends of the land
        in my disbelieving face

        don't be speaking to me like that
        bruising common sense blanching the common good

first thing out the mouth don't even have to be words
rapture scatting   praise faces beaming   good in you bending light in the room
illuminate *do-right* coursing in the bloodstream
of people you meet or children you raise

hmph   enunciate the first thing
        like you a duet partner with Sarah Vaughan

send in the clowns for real
laughter scatters red joy
baggy improvisation brightens eyes
music faces merry go round

like   what if the first thing sound like
           Muhammad Ali floating boasts on a summer cloud
           Sweet Honey blending out front a militant hum
           Malcolm pinpointing on a cushion of new-day Erroll Garner
           Mother wit guiding by the light of Ida B. Wells
           you yourself *being* to the core of daylight in your baby's eyes

what's the sound of the second thing   third thing
if the first thing out my mouth
wear on the ear with proof of an original tongue
what's the movement that follow
when you been touched by electric confidence
& been told ever so sincerely day-to-day
on a regular basis without even one request for interpersonal refund

you are a miracle wrapped up in human flesh

GIDDY-UP LOVE

(duet w/ Al Green's Love & Happiness)

giddy-up love
show me power eyes inflamed w/doubt can witness
laid children
laid family
laid women
laid money
laid time
at your altar
stood for you   stood up to you

bleed into me w/an R&B transfusion
dress morning sky in crimson when I pray
spread moss under my feet when I dance after sunset's call

marry me love
be good for me

laid mother at your altar
laid father
laid memory
laid faith
laid hope
tortured myself in your name
expressed myself without game

help me find my rhythm beyond blues
help me moan till I regain my sight

lay my tears
lay my loss
lay my want at your altar
lay my groan
lay my ache

giddy-up love
gallop out my nostrils
pull up to my bumper
wink at me
size me up
teach me rhythm beyond blues
show me power eyes witnessed your fame
cannot doubt

A Sense of Ceremony

build a shelter
from slats off slaveships
bobbing to the surface
of the rivers of memory
(lance rotten knotholes & cure wooden leftovers with our prayers
dripping from squeezing eyes of clove)

stitch a comforter
from petals falling
off the rosebush of sacrifice
(drape it over our sanctified bed & seal hems with the grace
rising from our embroidery)

to keep warm in nightwinds of withdrawal
pound spring mud & autumn leaves into a robe without chinks
& toss a salad of sturdy underwear & overcoats

call the
uncles
aunts
elders
from the cities & the countrysides

call the
Revivals
Sundays
Midnights
from the shade & the highways

brew a drink from muscle
beating within spiked pineapples
simmering over charcoals of enlightenment

mix a liniment from camphor
bleeding alcohol to knit muscles

ripped in fiery exertion of meditation
then try a little tenderness
& let the good times roll
into a panorama with a view
from a room with no blues
flirting through the raised windows
with Cha Cha eyes scanning the indigo skies

& we
you & me
uncles aunts & elders
all wondering what took us so long

to build this place
to stitch this comforter
to toss this salad
to brew this drink
to mix this liniment

then let the good times roll
into a panorama of tenderness
with a view from a room with no blues
flirting through the windows with rhythmic eyes
& second sight flying the indigo skies
clinging to the backs of soft-feathered birds
praising our blueberry walk
& the quiet belonging we feel
in each other's nourishing arms

we face our fear
haints sucking teeth unshelve the book
of sacred instructions for haunted lovers

we turn to the random chapter on a sense of ceremony
written in one take by a left handed griot
whose 3-D business card shows rising sun on the front
& Rahsaan Kirk blowing a seashell on the back

in that chapter it advises:

build a shelter from slats off slaveships
bobbing to the surface of the rivers of memory
cure wood with tears from a squeezing kiss

stitch a comforter from petals
falling off the rosebush of sacrifice
seal hems with perfume from a sanctified kiss

face haunted nightwinds with a salad
of sturdy underwear & overcoats
soften autumn leaves with spring in a flannel kiss

call the
uncles
aunts
elders
from the cities & the countrysides

call the
Revivals
Sundays
Midnights
from the shade & the highways

brew a drink from tropical muscles
boiling over simmering enlightenment
drink in one gulp & open your mouth to a scalding kiss

mix a liniment from backwoods alcohol
& fresh water from a graveyard well
rub it over ligaments twitching from a cayenne kiss

then try a little tenderness
& let the good times roll
a sense of ceremony
will be yours to behold

remember

try a little tenderness
& let the good times roll
a sense of ceremony
will be yours to behold

Come Sunday

wake up a failure
skin burning
first hierarchy imposed by my country tis of thee
homeless but for a case #
penniless in coin of my realm
loveless   lost   invisible to my friends
short of breath   shorn of touch
older than my fears   unfulfilled   dead on my feet
earthquake in my empty bed
a ward of my son
an enemy to rewards
illiterate except in apology
fluent in nothing but nearsightedness
doubt my closest sibling
rejected   undiscovered   last in line for love
a child as old as his dead mother
music frozen
revered by all blues & weary indifference
clinging   ignored   missed by every milestone   afraid of holidays
dreaming of mothers witnessing their sons
attacked by other mothers' sons & evicted by riverfront condos that
    don't allow families
Black boys on skateboards point their fingers through subway window
assassinate the Black man of happiness in rolling pantomime

too wounded by words caused
to heal from wounds received
too resilient to appear in need of healing
you too, Love, you too?
who knows better than you my tenderness
holes that need filling
future that will footnote this immeasurable second
of excruciating hesitation
misalignment
inability
to do nothing but cling to circles & sine waves

within my incompatibility
my incongruencies
a failure at learning history
a failure at everything except failure
whose child am I?
Black vegetarian with simple hungers   hope of a refugee
charmed by circle & sine waves
in greeting or touch or instrument
or greeting in the touch of hand on a cello or kora
sweeping failure into the song circling failure
centrifuge spinning
up against the wall
bottom drops out
we cling with no hands
ask our mothers
ask our fathers
why don't we fall?

WHEN THE BIG SHIFTS

for Melvin

this time   he was laughing about being an ashy brown skin boy
stepping into Baltimore's clammy summer
feet coated with film from public pool dressing room
eyeing black bodies to pick one girl swimming alone
whose tiddies & ass he could touch on the sly
acting like he was teaching her how to swim

this time   home for my mother's funeral   together again when the Big Shifts
in our lives like when I braced elbow at his pops' funeral   who else but him at the
airport   big brothers both fucked up about Ma's death   who else so hip & subtle
to glide into McDonalds before we braved my family home   daddy's paralysis & the
well-meaning chaos of every other aunt uncle cousin neighbor I never knew we had

salt on the fries   sting in the orange juice   laughing to keep from crying
smoking that cancer stick which just do not stain his bleached bone teeth
sipping steaming coffee on this steamy D.C. as in District of Columbia
Washington, D.C. kind of July day until somehow we back to being kids tapping
asses   I own up to fiending for Heidi the only gap-tooth Hungarian-sounding sister
in Parklands whose behind rippled under whatever dress or bathing suit or fur coat
she wore (rumor was she was a stripper by night)   told him my *jones* made me grab
when I should've grazed   palm when I should have hovered   how I made up lies to
knock on her door   found myself conveniently in her vicinity at all kinds of
adolescent hours

he chimed in   somewhere in there   after or before he stopped snorting
that high-pitched laughter of his   leaning his head back the way he does
thoughtfully spraying smoke just above my head
slowed my *blindbeating* with life before & beyond my inflamed sight

I want him to teach me how to swim
he reminds me I already know how

then again he got his eye on somebody else anyway
somebody who sits softer sweeter in a striped bathing suit
hotter even than Styrofoamed McDonald's kinship over coffee

THE BLACK MAN OF HAPPINESS

at City Crossroads
joy lift baggy clothes into smiling balloons
awe trailing like string dancing in the wind
all of our lives whipped into meringue by teenage recklessness
drenched with mesmerizing sight of love on display
holding hands like human beings unhinged from tragic theory

at the corner of win & lose
glorious passion waits for light to turn gold
riveting theater in their stroll
smoother than wheelchairs stopping traffic
stepping through crosshairs until crosswalk releases scent of cobbler

at unexpected intersections The Black Man of Happiness
catches stories right before intonation shapes words
stands in the flow that melts cataracts & shows hidden insistence
seized by the grammar of submission

                awed   porous   magnetic
Ptah   first island among Waters of Chaos
absorbing shock of creation in everyday lives
converting atom of thought into power & voice
released from rules of thumb by shifting voices within waters
whose guidelines subvert all rules
change the only mortar (or protection)
holding together life & death between the blues

                you know it baptized   sculpted
sifting pits & stems for fruit above waterline
legs wrapped around submerged roots
anchored   swaying in Mother Breeze of first meetings
shape of destiny rippling across democracy's mural still sweating on the back of
   his eyes
offering no explanation beyond the tingle of invention
fearing no weariness even within deep memory of being quarry for dogs & hysteria
consoled by ferocious humanity at the crossroads of creation & death

The Black Man of Happiness
voyeur translating the surreal privacies of our living metropolis
ID card a moody hologram tinted in everybody's complexion
face wet in witness to daily rites of passage
intoxicated by our sophisticated lives
naked with peaceful recognition
game to face dogs & hysteria
prone to find trails to safety
protected always by the commanding serenity
comes from wading with whatever the water brings
holding hands when a fist is needed
unclenching when it's time to just know what needs be known

10 Minute Prayer

uppity in God's chest

a place where nobody stands in line for love
everywhere
I can be on the fabulous end of a sister's eloquence
reward is stamina to celebrate
& our choice of theme music
exhaled from guitars
cooking with friction of our flirtation

floating in God's chest
a place solid as a 10 minute prayer
soothing as knowledge of water beneath land
everywhere
calming me at the news my daughter *enjoyed* her first sex
our reward is stamina to celebrate
& our choice of daring
laughed from chants filling days & nights without suspicion

I ain't being a man right now
an embryo in God's chest
my chromosomes are unnecessary
in a place where I am not a prisoner
my son is my mother
my daughter is my father
each moment a universe
wisdom burns on candles of sound

ember in bassinette
invisible shrine for an urban pilgrim
my, like, you know, *mumbling* understood
everywhere
cycles unfold smooth as shifting yoga postures

ember is stamina in my chest
a place where no child stands in line for love
& fabulous recipes of survival
are rewards at the receiving end of please   thank you   sho you right

ARETHA SIDE OF SPACE

who's child am I?
Black vegetarian cured of cravings for clove-scented death
baby galaxies behind my smiles full of cool young stars gathering
to convert a chitlin into a megaphone vibrating w/*cosmic* soul food
nourished in the home for our future   grail in the architecture awe connecting
rooms of glory blowing through ducts in every season   gratitude fluorescent in
the good mornings in the good nights galvanizing every family holding out for
evidence the common giggle can rivet satisfaction into the voluntary lifetime of
perspiration

mothertouch fathertouch collapse chitlin into worm hole
expanding end reveals future coalesced into intergalactic lamentations of Aretha
scooping nightmares from the chilled air twisting my torso from the fear my flesh
will forever be slapped behind bars   my ass forever strip searched in the middle
of a high school art class   forcing my teacher to choose between service as a hip
guardian or butcher's assistant

who loves a baby galaxy full of cool young stars?
each one conjugating light from my ancient birth
spinning delirium from the *All 'n All*
ain't no vacuum on the Aretha side of space
baby baby baby I love you
first rhythm of serenity after nightmares
bleed through deafness as the galvanizing evidence sustain us
so we can walk into any home
smell of blood soothing as memory of a familiar face satisfied with sweat   free of
threat & smirk of the missionary
place at family meals comfortable as tie dye
we feed on the gospel & protein of our interdependent lives
swirling like the milky way
will take us 200 million years to return to this one spot
but in our wake
skanking
like dancers at Marley's last concert
wishes upon a billion stars
promises we know Aretha's already kept

HORN SECTION

"Don't stick your head out the window
they shooting everything that glows"
— Nikky Finney

November sings in tongues through shivering trees
winter's tambourine stirs barbecued leaves
short day sundown
cloaks ancestral saxophonists
savoring tropical memory
perfuming the promise of hawk
soloing its biting *lullaby of dusk*
horn section for everyday people
Nana   Tío   Auntie   Cuz
hear tunes they want wind to play
to soothe ears stung by whine of
bell curved liars   english-only canters
Nordstrum scholars   one-note theorists
my own soundtrack echo King Curtis
blowing me a raspy escape route
out the box canyon of my mediocrity
fingering me a bridge to a safe place
where Bobby Byrd invites me to repeat after him
I know you got soul/if you didn't you wouldn't be in here
sitting in on the jam session of resistance
searching my instrument for one grace note
pure enough to bopgun frontliners who've exhausted their funk
            horn section
tuned & timed
to roll with
the ballbearing
needs
of any era
comping for the call to *hit me*
accenting pleas of a Vietnam vet on homeless knee
throbbing between fingers of men reciting the Million Man Pledge
praying she'll come back to me
stretching time while she meditate
strutting when she say *hmm hmm*

swaying when she hold me in her storybook arms
high-noon sprawling from an orchestra on the curve of a liquid sky
filled with soloists begging for the nod
to eliminate words altogether
ax angled like Prez or unchained like Trane
willing to leap into the wind or worry a toothpick
as only a virtuoso signifier can do the do
from mouth on machine activated by inspiration
vocabulary of sound daring us to repeat when breath
of turning seasons chill our intentions

I know you got soul/if you didn't you wouldn't be in here
I know you got soul/if you didn't you wouldn't be in here

CULT LEADER IN TRAINING

a drum major for spare change dragsteps
between lanes of us unleaded idlers
tired eyes eclipsed   stained palms pleading
any face I make will mock him
any coin I give will dilute his testosterone
exhaust fumes coagulate into a premonition of death
            any minute now
this how I'm going out   this brother here
snorting high octane paranoia   suckling through teeth
filed by a lifetime of grimacing trance partners
            takes it all out on me
unless I know a vowel   a consonant
unless I speak a tongue tied to salvation   each word
chopping a path away from oily avenue to startling example
two men exchanging grail to retool griefs

why can't the balm of our telling heal sores?
stitch rags into tight fitting parade wear?
straighten a tilted face into sober meditation?
flood known & soothing tales of faith into haunted lives?

me myself
I see us kicking it off
like two cats swapping sideline lies
waiting next down at the playground
laughing about how we used to dress
in sweatshop shirts with wideass lapels
tucked into slacks of cancerdyed petroleum
& still believe we was the finest motherfuckers
this side of a senior prom
embarrassed without embarrassment
digging into the sobbing pulse of phases
we go through to become grown Black men

I was 18
debating this Elijah-draped woman

a Players magazine dropped out the creases of my notebook
lay spreadeagle between us on the floor
Homegirl re-invented eye rolling
sighed a mini-prayer to Allah
sucked her teeth
I was president & a client of Infidels R Us

drum major hiss laughter through his teeth
wiping tears smear dirt off his fingerprints
he feel my everlasting moment
segue into his own memory like a FM DJ

his boys snatched him off the couch on a lonely Friday night
he was tired of clubbing truth be told
standing near the bar like he held secrets he ain't yet been told
he saw her   that one sister
with lowcut eyes   sunset in her posture
a neon thief who silence the pulse
could talk enough game herself
had him imagine
his lonely walk across a chaotic dance floor
really could lead to the end of a marriage aisle

I don't want this to end & it ain't even started yet
when it do
not one corny happy ending will cross my lips
at no time will his loyalty be the price for my gift
I will not exchange pledge for his prayer
I will always be a cult leader in training
forever subject to be upended by visions
of a boy phasing into manhood bending
to pick up a magazine filled with naked Black women

right now
I just want to breathe free of danger
right now
I just want to know
a premonition don't have to be nothing but a feeling

Bury the X

grainy FBI home movies
show Malcolm bottle feeding his unborn twins
X dissolving in giggles of happy
Black daughters suckling Playtex nipples
a playful icon
awed by humanity in his own likeness
unmarked by public declaration
each private moment a riveting call
to resist something   celebrate something
safe in a haven of his own simplicity
eyes tuned to each twist of his babies' fingers
ears swallowing the music of breast-fed breath
3 hunted bodies stealing a wisp of peace
haunted by images reflecting off hidden Polaroid cameras
& the sound of sliding doors with one-way mirrors
seeking escape from the echo of flying bullets

it is two days before my 43rd April 26
my own daughter's high school graduation is set for June 4
her 18th birthday one month & a day after that
college is on her autumn horizon
yesterday James Earl Ray died of conspiracy of the liver
two weeks ago Farrakhan hired a convicted X
who may been framed for Malcolm's murder
what vocabulary could resurrect good men & release them from the Cross?
allow them to see their daughters graduate into lives
free of the *what ifs* that shroud their days
would Malcolm be icon if he were only an anonymous father raising his children?
if his memory made us smell Brut aftershave instead of gun powder?
if his legacy was grounded on favorite bedtime stories instead of Ballot or the Bullet?

in the X-rayed faces of stark photographs
Muslim & Christian men
a Japanese-American woman of struggle
a pregnant mother unshielded from fascism

point to a staggering future as leaders
lay bleeding in their arms   at their feet
bullets unhinging the jaw of the preacher   excavating the chest of the Pilgrim
I am older than Malcolm   than King
grown men   fathers with great smiles   a sense of humor   the gift of story
60s' cats who loved sex   good music & the hip dances of their era
who had style & substance enough to galvanize public concentration
who had humility & courage enough to admit mistakes
to change in the wind of good ideas
to peep what was stale in themselves

there is film hidden in a psychic safe deposit box
film shot from a camera positioned behind Malcolm's pineal gland
film developed in the light suffusing Betty's proud face
surveillance tapes focused on orphaned babies waving to daddy they've never seen
film of a man spritzing milk on his wrist to check temperature of nourishment
called into being by the gravity of a father's love
luxuriating where X marks the spot of resistance & celebration

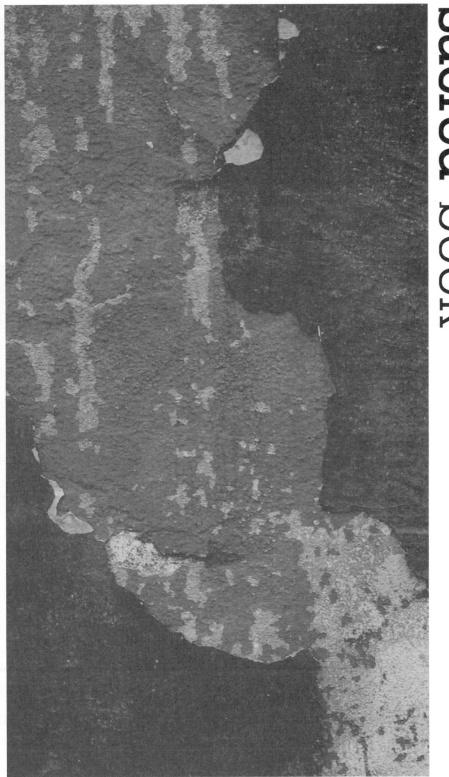

sacred book

Sacred Places Surrender to the Word

inside the mind or outside the senses
there are sacred places
where doors spring open from pressure of baby steps
where even squeak of hinges sound like Reverend Cleveland's all-star choir
where lives of asthma get resuscitated
& we can get on with the daily business
making the streets of our world
safe for men & women to double dutch in peace
slipping like sound between the bolo ties
waving & weaving at the wrist action
of girls with names that swing through the alphabet
there are sacred places
inside the city & outside the jails
where rules heal at whisper of first notes
where even demands of commandments fit like a one-off ensemble
where lives of sclerosis get massaged
& we can get on with the daily livelihood
making streets safe for men & women to play jacks in peace
counting sing song up past their tensies
bouncing little balls high enough
to gather scattered lives in one smooth grab
with the wrist action of boys combing hair
before a lint-free weekend date
there are men & women
with sacred places inside
who surrender to the word
without becoming vengeful
missionaries & crusaders
carrying spears & scimitars
& automatic weapons of conversion
unh unh to the word of ruthless invisibility
get to the word of the gesture
within the common smile the candy gesture
the gesture of peeled bananas
the word of the common reprieve

written without commission
from nobody's ruling class
from nobody's royal decree

inside borders or outside jurisdictions
there are sacred places
with doors fitted of spiritual carpentry
with rules jig-sawed of stone contemplation
where men & women are safe to live long as they supposed to
& die in their own unrehearsed moment
with another good idea perched on the lip
of their ever ready tongues

Bless the Ashes

I call on my June
January mother with summer name
I call on her New York voice freed from tracheotomy tube
to mash lumps of bad memories until I'm gravy again
I call on my June
to help me bless the ashes of my ripening
as I flower finally in the compost of her death & my heartbreaks
& wilted friendships flatlined after the smiles of lovers
became the leers of jack 'o lanterns
I can see her full moon face rise from handwriting that overwhelms the single
spaces of letters she wrote me on groaning legal pads
she is crying
my mother could cry & crown a moment with the majesty of grief
her tears welling from the whole residue of a life as a foster child
whose birth certificate said white & whose death certificate said Negro
she is laughing
my mother could laugh & soothe departure
her tears welling from the whole joy of a working woman
whose social security number said dependable
& whose Harris family addresses documented her refusal to pass

she is crying   she is laughing
wiping her nose with the same corner of Kleenex I handed her in 1965
her visit soothing me like the bath she drew to make my chicken pox stop itching
comforting me like her fearless kiss on my scabby soft spot
like the clean sheets she spread on my twin bed
she's come to dance with me on the Second Line winding back home
from her funeral

she says it's time to stop mourning
her death my heartbreaks & wilted friendships & her bedtime kiss
the ripped pages of her 20-year-old letters
the clink of quarters she handed me with orders to run downstairs and buy her a
chocolate sundae from the frozen custard truck with its tinkling bell
our Saturday trips to buy me the latest Fantastic Four & Silver Surfer comic books
even time to stop mourning the tough love

like that time she told me I would regret throwing away my John Denver records
cause I was a Black Nationalist promising I'd never again be Rocky Mountain High
& the afternoon she peeped unspoken frustration over my first marriage
then laughed & said "I'd hate to see you when you're *really* sad"
when I shouted through snot & tears that everything was fine
I was OK & why don't you mind your own business

                    she said it's time to stop mourning

start dancing
follow the bad ass band
playing the music for the ceremony that will bless the ashes
that got to be swept away
if we ever to breathe again after death & heartbreak & wilted friendships
start singing the songs blending words & music into perfect whole
spiced with the honesty of a brother inhaling the incense of his falsetto
& laughing out the blue when the lyrics fall from his mouth hit the sidewalk
& he hear background harmony swelling the cracks in the cement
covering the new American earth me & my mother stepping
wildstyling like the two converted wallflowers we are
saying fuck this standing around
let's dance this time   legs pumping like Ghanian women pounding fufu
let's dance this time   arms waving like church fans air conditioning
the Baptized skin of our Virginia aunts
let's dance this time   eyes closed trusting we ain't stepping on nobody's toes
let's dance this time   finding music in the pounding pain of our lives
let's laugh   let's hug   let's party
then turn to our past & speak

                    my bad or I forgive you

speak   keep dancing
following trail away from the funerals for every good that's ever died
naturally since I'm flesh she out of body
I ask
why I got to give it up like I got horizon on my forehead
why I got to have open heart surgery
with only invisible yes & sidewalk whisper as anesthesia
why can't I hold a grudge & swear on the shelter of calcified indignation

shit she don't even miss a beat   ask me

                    what do you stand for in the lives of your friends?

she point to ghosts holding up the walls we pass
they lining our path like Soul Train dancers forgot which beat to honor
they wearing clothes that make me think
it's the two wives I've left
children whose raising is pockmarked with gaps in time
it's the last lover who see her future without my touch
a friend whose hands turned radioactive on his woman
cause he couldn't say goodbye to her love
                              but they all wearing my face   they all me
moms turn to me
trach tube a rattlesnake in her throat
I hear her rasping funeral arrangements to me as I sit with her
in the ICU room at Greater Southeast Memorial Hospital in July 1984
I'm taking dictation
patient as she speaks
pauses to catch her breath
tries to rise on her right elbow
falls back
I'm taking dictation from my dying mother
asking for her Peter J the journalist the poet
to overwhelm the single spaces of the ceremonial journal
I was writing on the groaning hospital note pad
since I was her flesh she my mommy
I asked what we were doing
she smiled, wrinkled the horizon on her forehead
said "who else?" knowing I'd know she was right
this was my gift, not daddy's or big brothers' or little sisters'
this was my job
facing the ghosts
speaking for the ghosts
dancing with the ghosts
that's what I stand for in the lives of my friends

I see my new moon face reflected in her handwriting
I am crying
I cry & crown a moment with the majesty of grief
my tears welling from the whole life she helps me learn how to live
I am laughing

I laugh & hear her New York voice a symphony out my mouth
my tears welling from the whole joy she gives me permission to learn how to live

we unlock the door to the shelter of calcified indignation
my mother & I are living invitation
we joined on the Second Line by every me I've ever been
every good that's ever died is alive in our movement
                          it's time to stop mourning
follow the bad ass band
playing the music for the ceremony that will bless the ashes
that got to be swept away if we ever to breathe again
after death & heartbreak & wilted friendships
my mother say
fuck this standing around
the funeral is back thataway
live   keep dancing
speak   keep dancing
                      say my bad or I forgive
but it's time to stop mourning keep your head to the sky & tear the roof off the sucker

Don't Even Pretend
(The Saturn Poem)

From the Washington Post – November 13, 1980:
BRAIDED SATURN RING ASTOUNDS SCIENTISTS

PASADENA, CALIF., – "It defies the laws or orbital mechanics as I understand them but two components of the fifth ring out are braided," said Dr. Bradford Smith of the University of Arizona, one of the scientists gathered at the Jet Propulsion Laboratory to study photographs being transmitted from [Voyager I]. "If the distribution of these braids is uniform around the entire ring then there are as many as 1,000 braids in the ring."

Not only is the fifth ring in braids, Smith said, but the 500-mile long braids appear to have kinks in them. Smith said that as bizarre as the braids are the kinks are even more bizarre. "If you look closely, you see abrupt bends in the braids, as if somebody took the surface and bent it," Smith said. "I don't even pretend to understand what this means."

Saturn's rings was all nappy
spread out from her head
like she just woke up
took a shower & aint dried them yet
dread locks
cluttered with moons/meteors/mysteries
so god, She said:

"girl...now you know
I can't let you be orbiting round me
looking like that. suppose we have company.
what they gon think of me?"

God took off from work
unscrewed her Afro Sheen jar
washed her comb & pick
sat under constellations
& told Saturn to sit on the space
between Her legs.

"honey, I got to plait your rings
even if I miss a day's pay."

God got to cornrowing Saturn's rings

ain't nothing more coaxing than God's hands
spreading each ring into 3 strands
sifting through rocks that was worlds eons ago
She finger Afro Sheen down the part
softening scalp/loosening crusty moons
stuck in orbit
She start humming Nina Simone
while threading wisdom down each row

"here comes the sun
little darlin
here comes the sun..."

hands so knowing
they tug/twist/twirl those knotty rings
& Saturn don't whine
just listen to the lyrics
& feel tight lightness
creeping along her scalp
down her back into infinity
Saturn close her eyes
& feel peaceful
like when God rubbed Her palms
for the sixth time & rolled rings
from the swirls in the fingerprints
of each hand

"here comes the sun
little darlin
here comes the sun..."

God weave bright beads, baubles & shells
yellow curves/purple swoops/blue loops
decorate the arcs speading now
like the stiff necklaces
around the throats of Masai sisters

"there child. I'm finished!
my my, you look like a magic pinwheel
gracing space. Here, look in my corona
& see how pretty you are."

God hum & sigh
She got to rest these few more hours
work again tomorrow
smiling early from the east
glinting off Saturn's rings
like a fawn darting quenched from a water hole
and back into the forest

SON OF TWO FATHERS

for Richard May

boy fractured
dangling like a wish bone between
DNA   passion   vows
lovers' breath   holy duty   long goodbye
with each baby step cross a border
leave a father's song & shadow
diaper sagging under weight
of a name times three
carried by bow legs in search of a lullaby

sing father
sing step father
moan daddy
hum dad
blow pops

bow my teenager chin to chest
listen for family in relentless brilliance beneath my breast
blending lessons I learn in three accents
worry I am only epicenter of wounded people
crucible of festering emotions
hope I can become human moment fusing
into crisis resolved
moment stretched into a lifetime
illuminated by one mother loved by two fathers

a son
one man's biology
another man's life work
a son
curious within flames of fear
mysterious as his influences
hungry son

poised before
doorway to resistance
doorway to love
doorway to celebration

turn the knob babyboy
turn the key my man
pick the lock homeboy
oil the hinges brother
cross the threshold son

man whole
I am the son of two fathers
my shadow same as his
my hello echo his
my voice (1st father)
my handwriting (2nd father)

"When I grow up
I want to be just like my father
& the man who loves my mother"

the future is work enough
without devoting faith to yesterday's loss
need to reach horizon with now & then in harmony
child in me hold *everybody* responsible for the past
man I am say *let's do this now*
make the rest of our lives solid as Lou Rawls on a blues ballad

as funky
boy fractured
as unique
man whole
as timeless
pain healed

walk with me father
stand with me step father

hug me daddy
know me dad
live in me pops

like I live in yall
boy fractured
like I live in yall
man whole
like I live in me
pain healed

Night Around My Sleep

night around my sleep throbs with prayer
            visit me daddy
after five years out of body
tell me anything from eternity
six hours of sleep can contain
my young boy stubborness has leavened into grown man self reliance
pick up where we left off in December 93
I will listen with hungry serenity
surprise you with 100 proof curiosity

            visit me
now I lay me down to sleep
            visit me
I pray my father's circle complete
            visit me daddy

I am no mystery to you
you already know I give the finger to
Smirnoff Vodka billboards on my commute to work
I felt you standing beside me in Trader Joe's
when I said no to a bottle of Sangria as I bled
from the scalpel of loneliness sticking out my ribs
your loving whisper quenches my thirst for family
when I count like a string of cowries each of the 3,000 miles
I live away from our Stomping Grounds

fit me into your timeless calendar
I need this anniversary as much as I need
to hear your knock on my door
like those unscheduled Saturday mornings in Maryland
when your jar of decaf Sanka was the only stimulant in my kitchen cabinets
after your Beltway drive from Temple Hills to Silver Spring
you never drank a full cup of coffee during your visits
journey tonight from your place in the All 'n All & slip behind my eyelids
brew completion we can steep & sip & savor

one cryptic vision will reinvent me
one jump cutting story from before I was born
will have me kicking blankets to the floor
press into me the news in death
tongue tied circumstances kept from me in life

I want to memorize your unspoken voice soon as my eyes close good
   scold me
suck your teeth & say I told you so
   praise me
hum some Mahalia & hug me against your last goatee
   school me
twist your wedding band & unfold the quilt of compromise

wade toward me along banks of the James River
sit with your drinking buddies in that 62 black & white Dodge
steer your truck full of lawn mowers into my third eye
flash that sly grin gave me permission at 18 to say *motherfucker* around you
wear a flannel shirt with a fresh deck of Bicycle
playing cards peeking out the breast pocket
stand with steam rising from the naked skin you no longer need
like you stepping out a cool shower on an August weekend in a D.C. suburb

   visit me
show me the first steps of the dance Ma taught you
when she welcomed you to the waiting room of Paradise
   tuck me in with a silent lullaby
I will sing it whenever I sleepwalk
I will sway to it whenever I stumble
     in the frightening hopes of the rest of my orphaned life

LISTENING TO WONDER

They say that heaven is 10 zillion light years away
– Stevie Wonder

he stands on the 2nd floor balcony
wrought-iron thigh bracing him against
grief surging from open apartment door
mother of the dead daughter flattens her right palm against his breastbone
like declaring an oath before scale of *Maat*
poise in Prime Rhythm above balcony's edge

last she held his hand
he was in a coma pronounced dead by MDs
friends & family had covered his ears with headphones
when machines heated up with his Return

I told myself
you can't die
listening to Stevie Wonder

testimony irradiates her palm
laughter & humility expand his breastbone
pulse of life embraces this communion of the wounded
                man who rose like *Horus*
mother of the murdered first-born
                mute play brother

miracle is she pauses flow of mourning with her courage
to welcome condolences   swallow flames of unhealing skin

I grieve for Zuri
29-year-old mother
of 3

I claim Ketema
29 this September
3 daughters
V's baby girl
my knucklehead

first borns tied by death   life   friendship of parents
urban children w/African names
unprotected despite our executed prayers
our membership in the legislature of healing intent & humane politics
despite heeding our generation's summons to unwind from trance
& devote ourselves to sculpting an African American protectorate for children
born in 77 a continent apart   conceived in sex & love by bold cultural workers
seeking to realign their flaws & find meaning in Coltrane's bell   Verdine's bass
meditation after the Baptist sermon   vegetarian dessert after turkey dinner
Richard Pryor's insights after American one-liners

steeped in the impregnable tenderness of being brother & sister from
    different wombs
never a conversation without Long Tongue on each other's grown baby boys
    and girls
joyfully sweeping our tales & gazes over the contours of their fitful survival of
American violence until we got swept into urban whitewaters that Friday when
my voice mail amplified her shriek

Zuri's been shot in a drive-by and I'm on my way to the emergency room

6 months ago V bent over w/mysterious pains in her gut & upper thigh
MD reports that Zuri's fatal wounds overlaid exactly her mother's emotional
    topography

where is Stevie's resurrecting music now?
how does this mother still stand when a father becomes slag in agony?
jaws locked
without a word that means a thing
                        if it cannot reverse the report of
bullets screaming from the barrel of a Glock with illegal finger on the trigger
                        if it cannot thicken atmosphere into Kevlar against velocity
                        of lead
excavated by poor workers breathing below sea level
            if it cannot shield a nurse walking out a convenience store
carrying a bag of *chicharonnes* and a Sobe tea back to the car where her son stares
through the windshield as his mommy collapses on an LA street

what headphones can cover the ears of a whole country?

44

The Lost Song of Donny Hathaway

found on unlabeled reels
laying deep in the hidden pockets
of the Sunday Best worn by my mother & father
in their matching caskets

muffled music called out to me
just as the delicate ushers
began draping the veils & lowering the tops
over the cold faces of my parents
piano moaned under Donny's gospel touch
just as I began to drown in grief

I stood up
"listen," I said
the certainty in my voice
sliced through the ushers' official reverence
stopped the ceremony
I walked from my mourning bench
ushers stood aside like parted white curtains
I stopped before the bodies
of the immortal man & woman
who gave me my life
"listen," I said
driven by the aching joy of Donny's final voice
to ignore the reprimanding murmur
of the deaf bystanders

I unbuttoned my father's jacket
reached under my mother's blouse
I patted the tailored lining behind the seams
of his wool breast pocket
traced the path within the folds
of her favorite summer silk dress
I raised his still head from the satin pillow
lifted her stiff arms from her sides

jostling him
rearranging her

ignoring
challenging
the rising hysteria of the community of sorrow
disenchanted suddenly
with the No. 3 son
who always seemed
so cool charming & destined
to roll with the Kool Aid & caramel
of every catastrophe

even this one
even this one

I plunge right arm up to my elbow
into an invisible slit
open to the left of daddy's rib
my left arm is hidden
in a shadowy crease in the cloth gathered
at my mother's throat
I touch the pulsating tapes
& summon them toward the light of day

my head rings
Donny sings
harmony with the choirful of my parents'
advice told-you-sos jokes
preaching & encouraging authority
that bumrush my memories

a ribbon of tape connects the reels in my hands
I raise them over my head
mourners bite their tongues now
my erect back quiets the chaos I've caused
the minister waves the ushers away to their rigid places against the wall
the reels begin turning in my hands
the church singers stand
& without not one instant of rehearsal

sing their parts of Donny's lost song
the pianist cannot help but solo quietly & perfectly
the song brightens the dim rainbow of pain
arching over all of us
the casket tops slowly close
Ma & Daddy say goodbye through undertaker marble
widows rise to their feet
(they unveil themselves)
orphans feel peace of mind
feuding brothers reunite
distant sisters remember junior high commitments
old neighbors open their mouths with memories
of midnight card games & fellowship
during emergencies of life & death
the reels are turning
tape is looping over my head
& suddenly I know the story of the
lost song of Donny Hathaway

he was mourning his life
needing to be in places
that had given him peace
searching for the love
where is the love
5 hours on I-95 took him from New York to D.C.
needed to touch the D.C. in his past
the supper club on Georgia Avenue
the acoustics by the riverside
the echoes of the Southeast hills across the bridge
a place to sing the last song
where for years appreciating ears had smelted the early tunes &
the only feedback was rock steady applause & swaying bodies

who could be vessels for a final song?

handmade people
unafraid of their scars
fingering their seams & stitches without shame

well worn people   young & old
clothes out of style but draped in perfect fit
people sure that laughter & crying were the same thing
raised their own children & made
sons & daughters out of the friends
of their sons & daughters

man a beacon
woman a landmark

their lives pulsating so strong
that a melancholy composer
could hear & follow the evidence
right to our family home
where he knew the welcome mat was not bullshitting
& the fried chicken was greasy
but perfect for a traveling musician
in search of the right arms to hold him tight
where the meal was in the air
as much as on the table
where before he left
never to return
the tapes could be placed
in hands that made food grow from the city's backyard ground
in hands that made words march across wide savannahs of paper

since 79
I have always wondered
why I could hear rippling water
in my mother's whistle & my father's hello
until I heard the same surf
playing from the tapes turning & turning & turning
in my hands at their funeral
I pull down the reels
hook them on the sprockets of my nipples
with each revolution
song melt deeper into my skin until tape disappear
song perfume the chamber of death with reason for living

I open my mouth
sermon swirl among dedicated bouquets
flowers testify in swooping colors
exhausted mourners breathe again
church renewed within a shower of electrified petals
spring erupt from people's eyes
standing with naked joy on their faces
carnations sprout from the men's lapels
baby's breath dust the profiles of the women
children pluck falling roses & stuff their pockets with velvet
satin drape heaving shoulders & revival weep onto unstained floor

I clap my hands   steel pan exhale *jump jump*
I snap my fingers   tabla whisper *tap tap*
I roll my hips   cymbal sizzle *kiss kiss*
I blink my eyes   castanets come *chit chat*
I raise my hands   choir rumble *oooh oooh*
I nod my head   fingers coax milk from piano keys
rhythm flood my grief   rhythm full of peace

I turn around
my tears fall & hit the ground like tambourines
until there are no more strangers
& we pledge to face our next daybreak
waking up through all the pain
stomping on silence & through the rain
shouting the lyrics of our worthy lives & of our family names

GROOVED PAVEMENT AHEAD

born of sperm charmed as a look of love
born of ovum perfumed as a look of love

grown out the womb
drum major of joy
working class avatar
DJ channeling The Disappeared
mystic diagramming hearsay
enzyme of the Maestro
splendor of all favorite 'tings
The Apocalypsonian

—

—

voice pierce core of trouble
luscious with yearning of conch shell
breath scent of promises before they get pimped
hand-clap spark neon from fear
walk with velocity of ecstasy
stomp & serenade percolate through bedrock
asphyxiating path to Grooved Pavement Ahead

unveils synergy of laughter
three years of affection in each smile
hypnotized by syllables of baby talk
navel connects to all who have refunded atrophied breath
chants lullabies unlocking concentrated inquiry of our world

Who give you permission?
What you been shown to be?
Who your people?

—

—

empath to geopolitical emotions
refuses assigned role as local color to the police state
couldn't threaten a child if hexed by post hypnotic suggestion
seeks no entré into halls of marble contradictions
jumped off tongue-tied ship of history
peeps trickbag of power granted for a *martyr's* patriotism
stares down illumination granted by the wrong Americans
The Apocalypsonian shouts warnings that ruin their stake-outs

——
——

public servant with touch of ripe avocado
open to transfusions from all knowledge
humbled knowing land is older than humans

What's 100,000 years?
Who your people?
Who give you permission?

he could front as savior
recruit apostles to shade him with umbrellas
translate pronouncements on his species' stories
could be tempted to remind us all
(reverb of repression tainting his plasma)

I have never banned a people's language
snatched children from their culture's briar patch
slandered a Maroon
posse-pounded after a family running into independence
sewn passbooks into the seams of innocent citizens
fractured justice in Black Codes Fugitive Slave Laws Patriot Acts

resists tendency to swap curses
if we swapping gifts, well then, let's get scarlet up in here
fine-tune our surveillance
what's that sign?
Grooved Pavement Ahead

—
—

everyday to pay off debts from old lives
stay solvent & plugged into his era's configuration
The Apocalypsonian gig 8-to-5
tucked into his office he plays radio all day long
FM paints atmosphere with a second coat of confession
until rush hour brings him back to the crib
signs sprout alongside Interstate asphalt
wavy black slashes on yellow metal
warn of grooved pavement ahead
braised lanes where drivers might lose control because painted lines
lost that loving feeling & rubber shocks steering wheel

he strains to grip without drifting
Who give you permission?

lifts his hands
coasts in a ride precise as a tuned-up motor booty affair
finds him homing in on sights he sees with sore eyes
boarded up storefront of psychics & palm readers
pretentious sell-speak of billboards for overpriced cars
a homeless Black man pushing an overflowing shopping cart
five paces behind a lone Mariachi stepping with his loaded guitar case
tears condense into fog on rear view mirror

Who your people?

raw originality   sight & reach   rhythm & seed   hope & ritual
chord of human muscle

code for world peace can be sampled from banter
between James Brown & Bobby Byrd
a block party can morph into press conference
giggling children take questions
belt-tightening teenagers flash signs
that smelt grates on our doors into collectors' items
tilt their gaze to unscrew bolts on bars commanding our windows closed

What you been shown to be
when there's Grooved Pavement Ahead?

——
——

3-day GoGo of passion cell division carnivale
implode into the *tumbao* of his ecstatic life

on day one
gleaming Black hands cupped sunrise
trembled through the parting hours
hovered   descended drawn to combustion between man & woman
electrified by downstroke from all directions
gliding magic *perfuming* their look of love
igniting their seamlessness
Black hands cupping lovers
feeding them gravity of dancers orbiting invisible meaning

on the second day
9 blindfolded Monarch butterflies
fluttered against midnight
wing-to-wing in a sliver of sight through closed eyes
dropped & draped the cooing between mother & father
enfolded by sleep stitched from the velvet of satisfaction
butterflies alighted lovers' head-to-toe
wings droning with a choir's amen to life
annealing from the forge of relentless recombination

three days in
a riot of becoming in the vows of loved ones
circles fused hands raised guarantees to humbly protect this stirring
who will guide us through chaos & into Grooved Pavement Ahead

We give you permission   We show who you need to be   We your people

——
——

inside the womb
nourishing suspension   clavé of sperm & ovum   microscopic contusions   elemental
sequences   relentless radiation   human all at once   by time   by chemistry
by sensation   by skin & bone   nerves   hormone   skeleton   weight of muscle
crackle of reflex   serenade of brain wave

celebration an echo   speech an incense   song an invitation
to stretch through saline of creation   somersault into human with
all systems sealed by infinite calibrations

outside the womb
a balm of round-the-way home-training & esoteric passion
birth a key to ethical doorways
stands poised on the balls of his feet
first inhale, a pledge
first exhale, a grammar
first step, a freedom
second step, a direction
skin sensual enough for love, taut enough to know artificial touch
skin fragrant enough to announce arrivals
dangerous enough to scatter knuckleheads
savvy as a cat burglar reformed by vibe in a peaceful home
mind tuned to sort sacred & profane
balance momentum & stillness
sift opaque connections
reveal helix of Grooved Pavement Ahead

———
———

dancing on molecules of emotion
hips the gears of accelerator fueled by *ecstatica*
separating spectra into constituents visible through benevolent metabolism
rage balanced by strategy
revenge synthezied into reinvestment
self hatred overwhelmed by *well well well*
action unmoored from party politics
rebooted by a look of love

hearsay diagrammed:

between each beat Apocalypse is a temptation
each beat heeded offers the reward of Calypso

get hip to Rite of Passage in wood shedding
the percussion of water
sovereignty within & without the circle
virtuosity of the good idea
solitude of come what may

The Apocalypsonian... handling
too subtle to grant permission but definitions shine in his wake

The Apocalypsonian... reflection   promise   evidence

Grooved Pavement Ahead... *Mighty Mighty*
a mirage if you complacent   benediction on the soles of the pilgrim

Grooved Pavement Ahead... scarlet quilt   angled horizon   North Star

WITH OUR BABIES

put down your gun/*pick up your baby*
undo your collar/*open up your arms*
strip off your uniform/*salute to your equal*
unpin your badge/*reveal your rib cage*
dismount your Tomahawk/*hometrain your tongue*
swallow your mushroom cloud/*civilize your crosshairs*
put down your gun/pick up your baby

we hush children with full-clip seduction
check their fever with kerosene rags
dab runny noses with knuckles polished by crocodile tears
refuse to shed dead excuses
while our youngins killed in the line of duty

at the seance we must hold in atonement
I will enter the room wearing a collage of
drive-by camisole   carjacked khaki pants
a ghettobird overcoat   sneakers with Rodney King laces & neon heels
from my backpack I will pull bottles of holy water distilled at room temperature
a cassette tape of toddlers giggling at the silly jokes of serious men & women
a video tape of mothers & fathers smashing 40 ounce bottles & crack vials
whitewashing cigarette billboards & pimping through the halls of congress with
rehabilitated lobbyists

my skin covered with a tatoo bearing the names of children
starved by forgetful recipients of affirmative action
my third eye a hologram with the shifting images of pie charts
comparing government welfare for citizens & corporations

in the rotunda where we must hold the seance of atonement
the voices of the despised children will rage along the curves of the circular walls
the indignant agonized sound shredding the protocol of NRA mailings
interrupting the remarks of the Senator from shadowland   shattering the goblets
clinked in toasts of accomplishment   challenging our satisfied laughter
I can't just hold hands in the dark

(something is wrong with our babies)
the seance is over
(something is wrong with me)

I put down my gun
my collar is open at the throat
my uniform is a pile of cloth at my feet
my badge has been spun into piano wire
my Sam & Dave tongue bleeds the music of Earth Wind & Fire
through the crosshairs of civilization I read the stones of a kaleidoscope
when something is wrong with our babies
something is wrong with me

haunted lovers

15-Minute Moan

that's a 15-minute moan, set all your clocks by me
a 15-minute moan, set all your clocks by me
wind me up till *spring* get sprung
slow me down, make time freeze
                    (*take all the time you need*)

how long? long enough if you slow your roll
killing me softly when you slow your roll
every answer in just one long kiss
ain't no secrets you don't know
                    (*for you baby anything goes*)

Shhh ... my body ringing like chimes
whole body ringing like chimes
it's way past a respectable hour
your daddy must be old Father Time
                    (*do not start me to lying*)

                    finally let down my guard
                    again, again, like a cuckoo clock alarm
                    ride me in reverse, baby,
                    right back to the start
                    all the way back to the start

listen to that 15-minute moan, set all your clocks by me
a 15-minute moan, set all your clocks by me
wind me up till *spring* get sprung
slow me down, make time freeze
                    (*take all the time you need*)

CELEBRATING PASSION

Quite simply a poem shd fill you up with something/cd make you swoon, stop in yr tracks, change yr mind, or make it up. A poem shd happen to you like cold water or a kiss
— Ntozake Shange/Nappy Edges

brazen as a crack-pipe-selling traveling salesman
who scams a taxi driver, sneaks into my house &
draws a bubble bath in my claw foot tub   *foreplay like that*

face down in tangled Lotus flowers transplanted to a shallow pool in the Ever-
glades tongue kissing a crocodile drunk on Gatorade & thrilled he just escaped a
dare to sunbathe in the bed of a Prada pick-up truck idled by flat front tires
passion like that

relishing your wet sex chanting sea salt scented language of awe like a sommelier
graduated from high school in southeast DC   humble shoulders curved like a
Muslim bowing for 8th prayer of the day   fending off blue wind of low-riding
constellations insisting we shush this luxurious conversation spoken in the round
loving like that

when I fall back off your rippling glistening nipple
nodding like a swooning newborn
cradle the back of my neck   blow soft puffs of change into my mouth
hum a bluesy nameless lullaby until I see haloes of intimacy like linked Olympic
rings swirling slowly above your head   *love like that*

be like that
before I faint
chant my name in your nighttime voice   *raspy as Bobby Womack*
streaked with soprano only my touch summons
gloom all gone *like that/yeah like that*
tambourine shivering up & down our ovulating spines

Begging Is a God

begging is a god
underwear drooping around his peeled core
code initiated from down on his knees
hope found in temporary bravado
please please please prostrate at altar of deliberation
lips kissing up to cool skin of unknown answer

trembling begin my deliverance
believe my need for your Sunday throbbing against invisible evidence
beg for another exchange of serenade with no promise
we have enough oxygen to sing together
squint through prism of beginnings
hear each word unstained by experience
before sting of kiss
haunting touch
thoughtless voice
before need's seizure

begging is a boy drunk on hormones
his Hanes sizzling through wet dreams starring a god who never has to sing Doo
Wop   never loses erection   knows when to snap his fingers igniting music always
make a lover dance into arms that never quiver

begging sobers a man humbled by marvelous search for one human female who
is invisible evidence unnamed by any clergy   two-toned throb his elemental wish
& tongues tied only if exhausted by talk   blame neutralized into a carnival of
nuance & knowledge

order tested by faith in chaos & familiar danger of love
irresistible enough to dangle from swinging trapeze
frightening enough to initiate a god knocked to his cotton-candy knees

Right Now

I want you right now
I want to singe your lips
claim your shoulders
sip your heat
I want you alive inside me
pour your rum in my mouth
stretch your length on my chest
flaunt your style in my eyes
rain your twist on my hips
rub your moods in my beard
I want talk
        murmured celebration
        holy whispers
waves & waves & waves
        tender laughter
        tearful passion
hours & hours & hours
        fearless experiment
        stubborn excitement
years & years & years
        surprising mystery
        mysterious surprise
I want you right now
no hesitation   shouts & silence
no distance   stroke & smolder
I want to
simmer sizzle fry leap wade bathe
in the liquid of your kiss
sprawl skip flip purr breathe
the fine hair rising from your fine neck
I want to peel to my nerves
feel your massaging knowledge
tremble tumble
acrobatic stagger through the humidity in your voice
bow forehead at your *shadow's* feet

give   take   beg
moan open a vein
inject you straight
chased by healing I swallow
as you swell   roar   sigh in my flickering mouth
I want to head off all research
cut funding to nosy scientists
roll my eyes at any medication
prescribed to calm my nerves
Aretha got it right the first time
don't call me no doctor either
I will spill the syrup
lock pills under my tongue
dilute the cure
dance in my fever
crack mirrors with the madness in my stare
cut my feet
heal them walking in your footsteps
I want you right now
don't take out no patent on my patience
just take me in your arms
rock me   rock me   rock me
roll me   roll me   roll me
like an erotic chiropractor
playing my organ with knuckles & feathers
prancing to the desperate music
play with every crack of my slippery bones

YOUR BODY IS A MAGIC WAND

your body is a magic wand
you just standing up there blurs my vision
just you   standing up there
shifts ground underneath my feet
up there   just you standing
streaks sky with finger painting

roll your eyes
my incantations evaporate into steam
wave your hands then you turn me
into a flower in your chest
I'm in season & lovely
for special occasions

Billie's gardenia
fruit on the heads of market women
mysterious scent when you get dreassed up
red petals on opening night
grieving carnations at a teenager's funeral

your blood makes my thorns sprout
then you turn me into the man in your life
I'm adult & meaningful
weaned & Good-to-Go
I find the secret
make my own body a magic wand

I'm just standing up there
blurring your vision
just me shifting earth under your feet
up there   streaking finger paint across the sky
roll my eyes steam up your spells
wave my hands then I turn you
into the flower in my chest
you're in season & lovely
for special occasions

Billy Eckstine's boutoniere
sugar cane in the hands of field workers
mysterious scent when I'm in a mellow mood
lemon trees on holidays
cautious mistletoe over peace talks in the hoods

my blood makes your thistles bloom
then I turn you into the woman in my life
you are adult & meaningful
weaned & Good-to-Go

we find the secret

our bodies magic wands
we just standing up there
blurring yall's vision
just us   standing up there
earthquakes cracking yall's sidewalks
up there standing   just me & you
fingerprints streaking across the sky

then we turn yall into flowers inside our chests
we grow into evergreens above the smogline
stay there
until yall find the magic wand
in the briar patch of your own ribs

RIFT VALLEY GIRL

updraft from vacuum perfumed by beloved voices with names
too fragrant for sadness   sashay too fragrant for wavering
want my wisdom partner   intuition slinging between us
want tradewinds heated by cradled kora
& balaphone's incantation coaxed from anger's adolescence

want my blues on an oud
wake up with me   telepathy aint articulate enough
hear my single string corrido
jali's intonation
want my need released by grito

finger me like kora strings
pour me within spaces of balaphone keys
ply oud of my skin
wail your tale in my corrido   riff on my grito

                              Rift Valley Girl   Rift Valley Girl
history of love before slavery's invention in my beloved call

                              Rift Valley Girl   Rift Valley Girl
words exchanged compost on floor of radioactive chasm

steep loss
perfumed by hint of names
too fragrant for sadness

want my salvation aged in perfect ache
belly dancing with her in the crucible of crosswinds

ANOTHER SUNKEN TREASURE

*"going down to your river makes me shiver
and the chill of the water feels so good"*
—Nona Hendryx (for LaBelle)

I was in aftershock
when her voice seeped through my faults
"see what I did: I caused you an earthquake"
she kissed my vital signs
calmed my shuddering
lured me out my coma
I opened my eyes on a natural resource
& thought
"I need a river in my mouth"
I explored her shores
came face-to-face with the source
she was a monsoon
when my voice surfaced through her wail
"see what I did: I caused you a tidal wave"
I kissed her flooded islands
calmed her whitewaters
lured her out of her fog
she pulled me on top of her
strapped her life vests around me
we drifted to the peaceful river bottom
our duet another sunken treasure
we slept beneath stilled waters & satisfied earth
we slept beneath stilled waters & satisfied earth

THE NEXT STEP...WONDER BECOMES KNOWING

~ ~ ~ ~ ~ ~ ~ ~ ~ ~ ~

the next step sanctifies my stillness
the next decision transforms my sleep
the next memory bypasses my lifetime
the next peace encodes my knowing

~ ~ ~ ~ ~ ~ ~ ~ ~ ~ ~

the woman I love wakes with the dawn
burrows into my sleep
braids frayed, she nuzzles my throat's familiar sanctuary
she returns to me haunted by cries of humans packed in ships
feet damp from walking on braided seawinds
in a hoarse whisper, old tales of sadness escape
she remembers forgotten pain of heaving bodies

I am familiar with the hissing dream
fret within my own shrouded visions
unravel from our nighttime cocoon
with my hands gritty from crawling through upraised sands
I return to her grateful for sanctuary
in her curved hips warm back & murmured welcome
REM-broken touch is soothing tide after our nighttime excommunication

~ ~ ~ ~ ~ ~ ~ ~ ~ ~ ~

we had nowhere to run
            nowhere to hide
footsteps collared our ears
screams froze our thought
fear wilted trees & bushes
lush green flaked brown
parrots fell from branches
toucans flew in backward circles

snakes strangled on their second skins
monkeys shrieked out warnings
antelope rode cheetahs bareback

only Touch & Frightened Pledges
only her voice calmed me
only my voice settled her
when footsteps & curses
became faces became hands
became her face
dark sweaty gone

~ ~ ~ ~ ~ ~ ~ ~ ~ ~ ~

what I feel lives within stillness
what I remember lives weighted with lifetimes
what I cherish wakes me from my sleep
what I harbor lives without my knowing

~ ~ ~ ~ ~ ~ ~ ~ ~ ~ ~

timidly we accept our hazy recognition of each other
I hear her calls before she speaks
she completes snatches of spells I recall
something's familiar about the way she tilts her head   dangles
her hand
she knows how unexpected tokens make me shy

~ ~ ~ ~ ~ ~ ~ ~ ~ ~ ~

last night when we hugged
we rocked & rocked for a little while
air cooled around us
seabird feathers brushed our skin
sound of oceansurge echoed each endearment
initiation songs hummed in the tunnels of our throats

rhythmic creaking from waterlogged ships
slowed our momentum
our wonder floated like steam opening our senses

chains
we squeezed harder
chains rattled
we stopped breathing
seabirds
tears dripped into my eyes
seabirds cried
ache connected our lives
waves
someone whispered in our minds
waves roared
two voices answered at once
wood
"I will never leave you"
wood creaked
"then I won't be afraid"

~ ~ ~ ~ ~ ~ ~ ~ ~ ~ ~

breathing hushes away revelations
wonder becomes knowing

1,000 O'CLOCK

it is 1,000 o'clock
we splash in wet seconds of eternity
birth on our valuable breath   pleasure our midwife
your palm flattens my stomach
I undulate like an appointment w/ immortality

> your touch makes me forget
> I'm always a breath away from needing
> an undertaker's business card
> holding me like a sculptor cradling stone
> got me walking point at the tip of rejuvenation
> we in the place *spring* go for R&R
> this ain't just renewal   you make me *undam* myself

it is 1,000 o'clock
my skin is haunted inside out by your taste
I am sanded by your brilliance
I could not be clever if I tried
I stagger mute in your stare
your excitement in my ear indents me
desire for you the only constant in my life

now my time come to moan into the electrons
I stop asking *"what's my name?"* when I'm in your pussy
"what's your name? what's your name?"
w/ each rising reminder my ID falls through the trap door of memory
whose child am I?
a hard man to love right now   loving myself so hard
shimmering into the man I want to be
shifting till I can stay dry strolling through falling rain
weaving words into *do* recalled by my third cousin's children
standing up
wobbling under weight of my failings in a world
where baby Sherrice's life gambled away in a casino's videotaped toilet stall &
police step off prime time TV w/ guns enforcing US immigration policy while
Mumia can't get a minute in edgewise on NPR

standing for myself
bleeding but breathing to dislodge the splinters of citizenship
& finally feel the acupuncture of a balanced life

you read all this from the look on my face
as the fabled midnight hour melts into 1,000 o'clock
when I no longer know myself without you
                    you are inevitable to me
            I am susceptible to your shake rattle roll
          surely as I am to Earth's orbit rotate wobble
          speak my name & retune oscillation of my cells
          turn in your sleep next to me & align my spine
                against new morning's intimidations
                        counsel me in crisis
                    listen to my vulnerable voice
                    crave my sweat tears cum
            resuscitate amazement in every breath I receive

I know how to tell time
I know what time it is
it is 1,000 o'clock
I fear love but I ain't afraid
I know this moment is right on time

If We Gathering

if she say
shaping testimony & seduction
with words startling as snow flakes

if she terrified
dangling over chasm between
exhausted story she told old flames
& intentional original uttered for my ear only

      she gather me
      ripe hibiscus flower of a man   flush with willingness
tiptoeing through regret like a FAMU drum major
& bitterness become yesterday's ho hum
      she gather me
      resilience rocking us like a cradle
lined with a cushion of knowing
stitched together by unfolding divination

if she do
steady weaning me from potential
with demonstration classic as Etta James
she can say
      stand here
      sit here
      lay here
damn if I won't shift weight
like a background singer know all the steps
confident of my time at the mic
when she will suspend her control
for the riddle of trust   the effervescence of give & take

      if she say stand here
look at me trembling but expecting gone ground found
      if she say sit here
look at me fidgeting but believing she ergonomic

if she say lay here
look at me sweating but sizzling into place

if we true
negotiating know-it-all & invincibility
consummation conceived in the umbra of our lives
we gathering
lovers
even riled rested   tapping mystery
even scarred better
religion in the straining
conversion in the making

if we gathering
we say   terrified   true
we do

stutter shred vows I take too seriously to fake
freeze *whatever whatever* you been immunized against since high school

hesitation my shield against your summer weather
siphons pleasure from our sex
more scared than authority in my foreplay
old questions drape my fumbling
as revealing as lingerie you never wear

in this season of clear possibilities
I am without umbrella or handbook
my imperfections get coy on me when I question
whether I can convert communion into partnership
so incredible with me up in here alone
squirming against a Kirlian image of your perfect agitation against my body
& your ideas affirming as miracles
night ain't bringing sleep
mirror ain't reflecting answers
guitar riff & David Ruffin's voice
soundtrack for what my body know
i'm losing you
no matter that pleasure is a hurricane between us
our exhaustion oxygenated by your child's breathing outside this room
& I swear on the risk you are taking
trusting me naked under your roof
when I've admitted my 45-year-old wish
that it be only two grown folk swallowing each other
safe in the privacy of a home with walls decorated by pictures of our children in
college or raising their own kids alongside a portrait
of all us found balance in chemistry of mutual satisfaction
in a room painted a shade sweetened from the pigment of our blues

even now
with my *yes no i don't know*
a splotch against your guarantee
to work & walk with me

with my distance
stunned by your desire
to be & blend with me

if you touch me
if you touch me
you won't wonder
if you have   if you have   *you have*
if you do   if you do   *you do*
you won't doubt my passion

you may call me on my story
curse my dissonance
lament timing of our recognition
refund your pledge
but you won't wonder
if you have   if you do

if you listen
i am sound of crucified guitar & electrified anguish
shadowed by the standards of love
aint too proud to beg
but paralyzed by the knowledge of confirmation

who is this impotent man wishing he was a virgin?
who is this digitized man twisting away from your laser?
who is this radioactive man still searching his half-life for what's pristine?

orphan at the crossroads
don't know destination *irregardless* of which direction to take
craning for guide to walk this chicken across the road
choose a fit pair of hands will caress me until I'm strong enough
to share worry & story again
stutter smoothed into vow again
whatever whatever like a homecoming date again

without doubt
if I have   if I have   *I have*
if I do   if I do   *I do*

ANCIENT CIVILIZING SOUND

"are you sure, sweetheart, that you want to be well..."
—Salteaters, Toni Cade Bambara

I know   *what it be like*
to hear ancient civilizing sound
to know answer   *what you know good*
to feel you   carbonation in me
indescribable antiseptic for the sorrow below the surface of my skin

to crave ancient conversation revealed
within innocence of unexpected daylight
between umbra & eclipse battling below the surface of my skin
you listening inside crevices of my stubborn liabilities
a capella against frozen joints of happiness
& my desperate desperate intention to be well   to be well

what it be like
courage in every corpuscle
to emerge from the artery of the planet
examined by the ultimate physician in our cells
effervescent liquid excommunicating any traces
left of the sorry deep below the surface of our skin

your breath between story
unspeakable pauses   so ripe   so ripe
between the naked minute of my life so far
& the brave promise of crescendo
for the rest of my days

I intend
to be well   to be well
without desperation

I intend to be well
plunge into ancient antidote
feel the sorrow foam out of me

new tissue washed by inflammatory blood
& the excitement of this glorious stumble
an unchained marrow dance with you

BABY TALK

for Cecilia Woloch, Carmen Palmer, CarlosJuan

baby talk with assurance inside my labyrinth
softens crow's feet   silkens staccato within   unearths sprawling oasis where she
doesn't have to hopscotch around land minds   I don't have to tap dance &
 sidestep trip wires   beautiful detour on waves radiating from the bell we've rung
lines on our faces flare into delight of toddlers swooning to their trapdoor
curiosity   as we glide away from astonishment
& back to the world

decoded signs phase into view
inspect the promise of oasis be somebody's memory
be somebody's fragrance
is that honey perfuming the dashboard?
is that Bobble head Papa Smurf

dancing salsa in the rearview mirror?

CRAZY

Calypte anna, Anna's Hummingbird: males can be observed performing a remarkable ...
display dive ... he rises up approximately 98 feet before diving .... As he approaches the bot-
tom of the dive the males reach an average speed of 51 mph ... and produce a loud sound
described by some as an "explosive squeak" with his outer tail-feathers

what causes a hummingbird to strafe a man
strolling into Tuesday morning's melancholy?
poke out articulating straw of tongue & threaten to squirt nectar into his face?
dart toward a wrinkled forehead as if homing in on a homecoming nest?
hovering hovering in tiny invitation to an ecstatic chest-bump
a man jolted out of uncertainty by vibrating feathers
discerns his own initials inscribed on a miniature gold tooth

can a man on a daybreak constitutional be already exhausted?
be comforted by invisible hum of a tree full of pollinating bees?
stop long enough to sway to pulse of agitated blossoms?
sharpen stare to slowly focus on rump-shaking individuals?
hovering hovering in delicious concentration & indivisible industriousness
perched just within lips of petals trembling in ancient irresistible exchange

lingering lingering a man hears call & response & resolve
between hum of his own moan hummingbird's thrum & bees' ostinato

a man full of rage & sorrow
senses enough residual splendor in a new day
to calibrate delicate fist-bump with purple flutter
drawn toward stubborn fragrance of grace clinging clinging to him
reads a butterfly's flight path
as if it were dew-covered musical score
laid out by Miles Davis at first session for Kind of Blue
accepts anointment of Tuesday morning's call
to walk with Home Boys flexing their wings
before wading into administrative demands & practical hungers

their consultations
making more sense
than any advice

since his mother insisted
that doing the right thing
even when she was cross-town at work
in a commercial real estate office
would keep trouble away & carve out a path
that when orchestrated
would initially off-put anyone listening   scar even his own ear
for years to come if that is he ever found its flow
amid dilating compounding distractions
come with living long enough to look back in wonder

but keep listening
she promised
you'll know you're on point
when talking to yourself
& answering back
start making so much sense
you'll hear startling confirmations from the strangest places

Crazy, huh?

SITAR OF MY TOSSING & TURNING

Vasectomy Dream

her face shaped from stubborn cell division   plaits cornrowed from doubledutch
strands   eyeballs coiled wishes   eyelashes erased cilia   overalls stitched from
unborn hopes   fingers marked by scalpel   witness resurrected from sacrificed
shadow   babysteps creak floorboards spilling from rest-broken watercolors
voice embedded in atomic resiliency

who taught her to speak?   how could she know the sitar of my tossing & turning?
which lover her mother?   when did biology extrapolate into girl holding my hand
on a long stairway   guiding me toward sounds I recognize as a summer-night party
when I sit beneath dining room table lulled by thump of hands banging cards & my
father's inimitable shit-slinging in a bravura game of bid whist?

how could she make flesh & phantom fingers fit & polished steps materialize &
my pops slur his vodka-soaked Saturday revelry?   how could she wet my bed with
tears daddy withheld from his own mistouched daughter?

baby girl is a hula hoop of doubt & worry around my waist spinning into
diminishing undulation   my innocence & never-made memory scarring the
night   my purest child   vanishing from unopened eyes   fluttering to scenes of
fat cheeks satisfied by smile   damp hair tucked between my neck and shoulder
wet thumb held up for me to suck

she still sleeps safely in empty bed of man who chose genetic silence
somehow drawn to me in confidence   maybe after that night she peeped in the
glare of a late-night TV screen her teenaged sister tell me to *"slide over pops"*
before crashing in peace beside man divorce sucked from her daily bread

who favors right side of the bed?
snatches blanket in the scary part of the night?
who wet the sheet?

father & daughter rising & falling to xylophones in the wind water on it

CONTINENTAL SHELF

Ring Shout on a continental shelf
timing of a geyser or amniotic sac
submerged stomp over the edge
      here we go again
channeling panic at a runaway government
into thunder push up mountains
vexation transform individualism into a coalition's
predilection to get down on the upthrust
knee-deep in subduction between executive order & constitution
tectonics in our testimony against annihilation
discussed with indifference of a knock-knock joke
air bubbles like underwater flares

     who's there?
we submit to earth's governance of our Turns
but heirs to legacy of unbound memory
we deep weeping & honor bound to channel panic
into drum major's flamboyant echolocation

read the popping bubbles of our insistence sing echoes of our inspiration
hold hands with your ancestors survive on their water-logged *go head on*
bet with evolution
     here we go again
reforming the circle of shoulders on shaky ground
stomp & reverse a whirlpool high enough
to saturate beams from Star Wars
consecration unleashed from the sky   contemplation underwater
we wake in sacrifices of emissaries carry ID at gunpoint
reshaping contour of our own historical wish
       names bursting mouths
       ricochet branding hips
       consensus unlocking jaws
Ring Shout on continental shelf
timing of geyser or amniotic sac
risking quick step on H_2O
who's there?
who's there?

The Ocean Is Ours

don't be foiled or fooled by the zip code
the ocean is ours
the mountain is ours
the river is ours
the forest is ours
the sky is ours
anything less   no
to anything less   no
to anything less
than horizons & freedom & justice
    & peace & humanity
day in & day out   day in & day out
flooding the calendar with
        holidays & democracy & festivals
& meetings & resolution
I'm down with that   I'm down with that

don't be tempted or trapped by the zip code
health is ours
wealth is ours
government is ours
law is ours
safety is ours
anything less   no
to anything less   no
to any murder disguised as deterrence
  any whims disguised as policy
  any mercenaries disguised as leaders
  any theories disguised as gospel
  any gossip disguised as science
day in & day out   day in & day out
flooding the calendar with
        baptisms & rebellion & ceremony
& protection & institutions
I'm down with that   I'm down with that

don't be stamped or seduced by the zip code
the second is ours
the minute is ours
the hour is ours
the sun is ours
the galaxy is ours
anything less   no
to anything less   no
to anything less
than food & shelter & work
    & family & life
day in & day out   day in & day out
flooding the calendar with
       vigilance & fiestas & militance
& dedications & cooperation
I'm down with that   I'm down with that

BETWEEN THE WATERS

sit between the waters   temperamental mediator splashing time & dimension
splaying air   spooling memories   waterfall asylum soothing percussion of
the past   serenity promised in a fountain's cascade   splicing spectrum into
meditation's light

sit between waters sprayed from history   hosing me down   washing me down
hands raised against inundation of my palms cupped stubbornly to sip from the
rushing   soaked in the humidity of change   shaking me down   wearing me
down   stolen waters   poisoned waters   fractured waters   bitter swallow of
rusted waters sprayed scalding from radioactive hose & searing half life of mob
violence

dragged beneath waves   of voices tinged with oppressive accents   between back
seat & ghosts at our doorways   foaming dogs sicced by snarling civil servants
a stepfather shrouding bedroom thresholds   smearing the future with hands
dipped in poisoned heavy water   no no no   wash your hands   bend into
whisper of the water   sound of your grandmother visiting between the H $_2$ and O

sit here a minute   hypnotized by intimacy's pulse   behold the molecular tension
of good & evil   inhale raw oxygen   awaken like the signal of ignited hydrogen
etched by voices of dues-paying relatives   bathed between ancestors & elders
rocked in their subatomic bosom   expand & contract   dark matter caressing
your face

*sit here baby   how you living?   who you loving?   who's loving you?   don't let nobody steal
your time for love   take time to talk about love   sit baby   linger child   safe within
water's thunder   slip into the will of the waterfall right now   sit until you saved &
breathing underwater*

between cloud & aquifer   between a daughter's tears & laughter   dissolve into
cleansing emptiness   be born   vast   blind   translucent   spilling H $_2$ and O   *yes
yes yes*   liquefy liquid   drink me down   follow me down   carving crevices in
fossilized pain   sipping honey seeping from petrified victory   raise your hands
conduct the water   orchestrate out of chaos   geyser above the surface   sculpt the
future with the force field of your spray

WATER DRUMS

clock strikes 1,000 water drums call inundated memories split into molecules
cleaving to names initiated in long sutras of libations generations gone surge
into generations come fission of time spilling blues over rim of carbonated
rhythms releasing energy to dance under water rise against submersion & lean
into wind smeared by swirling mud

it is 1,000 o'clock water drums keep time this is how we make earth turn faster
on journeys promising sanctuaries where stained glass filters sunlight even at a
child's funeral harnesses chemistry of explosions whistling through hard-won
happy endings rallies us somehow water-marked awed that we still hear the
drumming between us

10-minute prayers douse flames & fears within danger's accelerator immerse
believers into the centrifuge of water singing splashing surviving persistent
breath breaks surface spiraling upward into sanctified atmosphere spun in all
directions like blues exhaled through a conch shell choir ebb & flow of Voice-
Music salting history with our startling names

Water Is Wide

Arriving asymmetrical Ashé *always arriving*
Ashé of indivisibility *transfigurations insinuated*
penitent singing the oblivion troubling the hymnal   celebrant witnessing his
first-born freestyling through reserved space of parted legs   salaam in our birth
cry rinses failure from genealogy   offers shelter in seasons of brooding *arriving,*
always arriving hurricane smashes thresholds   wind sweat leaps levees cheated
like sharecroppers   hungry baby rocked to sleep as poisoned waters recede
arriving, always arriving

chancing insinuation *winding, always winding*   rites carved from passages of
curving music *winding, always winding*   unexpected holy places at the shifting
crux of tragedy *curving, always curving*   sinuous as wind tracing trunks of olive
trees   sensuality of the oil & daring of rice terraces on a mountainside *weeping,*
always weeping at the beauty striating all chasms of pain *haunting, always*
haunting   sacred journeys through indecipherable signs hinting of unexpected
brush arbors *otro lado*

we are always arriving   navigating between every between   sworn to beneficence
beyond apparition *winding, always winding*   olive trees nourished by fallen fruit
rice terraces merging with million-year-old stone   weeping for the indivisible
songs of fallen serfs *working, always working*   asymmetrical as the penitent's Blues
dampening leaves of the hymnal

THE GOOD DANCE

for Reggie Wilson/Fist & Heel

contemplation in synch with acoustic tenderness   selection in tempo   slow
locomotion through rite of passage?   vamp to electricity of cleansing overflows?
reminiscences in stationery orbits?   beauty summoned & sifted from space
between fist & heel *body as holy book*   damp pages torn in the storms
torn from the storms

slosh of bilge water in a bottle drained from return voyages to Spain to England
walking on waves buoyed by precious memories   debilitating echoes in voices
of barefoot children begging tourists in 21st Century doorway of a 16th Century
cathedral

lightning flicks from dangling pinkie   skin taut by textured undulations
winding hips of alchemy   breezy flex cools dirty rice plié   gestures buttery as
Aunt Haley's Sunday biscuits   Sacred Secrets palpitating like last-minute spice
powdering the dough complexion of suavest acrobat   muscle threatening to pour
away from bone

honey, don't gulp down your ice water   button up your life vest & remember to
share your recipe with Jesus   can you turn open this bottle top?   that whisper?
Oh, baby, that's your grandmother visiting her kitchen between the H $_2$ and O

DELIGHTED HE COULD PLAY GOD

lopsided boy
arms brushing knobby knees on scarred toothpicks
jagged hairline shielding chip-tooth grin
dives into pool
tide swells in my direction
he is axe hacking water
his wake wood chips fleeing the blade

we sit breathing on pool's edge
what's my name   my job
why you swimming alonelaps at the Boys Club
craving inundation of my own son's interrogations
before his voice fades into court-ordered fine print
where is this boy's daddy or mommy?
I am brooding Olympian exhaling annoyance

his barbed wire smile draws blood from my solitude
he bends over water

you wanna see me make rain?

he cups his hands beneath sloshing surface
flings a shimmering glob above our heads
fluorescent light spliced by chlorinated crystal ball
mood indigo diluted into distant thunder
April shower splashes wet notes of balaphone against rippling aquamarine

he giggles
delighted he could play God
bless me with his joy

Tonight's California Rainstorm

tonight's California rainstorm
so freaky
newspapers sell front page postcards
(lightning licks bridges/brightens Marin mountains in the background)
so unlike the Bay Area this time of year
September being a month long sunfest
(sort of a Pacific Standard Time in the summer weather department)

tonight's California rainstorm
so contradictory
wakes me   lulls me
scares me   awes me
child in me wants to burrow under covers
run naked in swarming rain
man in me wants to swallow cloud burst straight no chaser
listen for thunder beat meanings

should just lay here
count stunning shudders
await blinking of flashsky
I think on this trying summer
flying back east 3 times to Ma
searching a judge's robe for my children's smiles
should just go out on the front porch
stand naked on top step
drink night spray through my pores
I think on hopes charging me
float a chain breaking Spritual on the virgin hour

darkness in my dry house
warmth in my dry bed
I breathe satisfying rustle of the nighttime
tonight's California rainstorm
my private lullaby
wordless
soothing
raging within ink dark clouds
between midnight & morning

The Promise that Twilight Made

twilight already promises
a night that would be a night
when all the holy statues
could wipe the tears from their eyes
when all the hopeful lovers
could hear a serenade of prayers
just from the water color evening breeze

      then on the dying spin of one long day
      floats an oldie by Billy Stewart
      the harmony of a new dimension
      reveals the promise that twilight made

just from the breezy water color
dripping music from the rippling horizon

      (I do love you/yes I do)

& it becomes a night
all the dry-eyed statues
tip from their santuaries down
to this seashore & sashay cross the purple seawater
Billy Stewart sings sweetly down by the seashore
clouds step across the sky like back-up singers
full moon glows like a church soloist wearing quilted spirit
Billy Stewart sings sundown by the seashore
lovers nod to his Doo Wop serenade

      (I do love you/yes I do)

      twilight died on the spindle of one long day
      all the holy lovers found a home
      in the watery folds of robes worn
      by statues swishing on the waves of wishes
on a night that became a night

when all the world's dancers
closed their eyes & swooned like newborn lovers
into the twilight water colors
dripping from the rippling places
where water meets tomorrow

LIQUID SCRIPTURE

liquid scripture thunders from melanin pools swirling
between the mountain range of my eyes
ancient lives blossom from touch of uncurling fists
spray of falling seizures caress our shoulders
resuscitation splases our skin
naked as headwaters
distilled from first true love
blended with tears after first goodbye

trickle all grown up   human waters surging from luscious combustion
hidden strain washed downstream   liquid scripture within healing danger
bottomless Black Pools excavated from my hard head
gaudy transparency melting gaze of my rugged eyes

just a sip at the lip of intoxication
just a glint off the hip of supplication
renewal wetter than rain
clean as our faces break surface of fear

we drink from torrent of falling our heads
bowed & baptized by weight of tender plunging tender

Water On It

put some water on it   hip scripture

say-so for the tests in my life
moral told in the Sacred Book for Haunted Lovers

put some water on it   riff worship

tap root for the rest of my life
gospel from throats fed up with constriction

ache on it
tremble on it
trust on it
swallow on it
surrender on it
put some water on it

gauze on it
massage on it
listen on it
muse on it
incense on it
put some water on it

quilt walls of the marketplace with Adinkra cloth
so a panhandler can interrupt without tiptoeing & adopt
the satin stance of somebody rediscovered the corn of life

put some water on it

giddy-up love
let a new season's sting purify the tears of life

glide on it
swear on it

sail on it
roll on it
celebrate on it
put some water on it

detonate a pot full of kale bubbling with the code of life
mainline dessert to human beings starved between the teeth of life

put some water on it

       seep into a country's DNA

remember on it
hunger on it
breathe on it
vow on it
stand on it
put some water on it
put some water on it

complete already

Always a Black Man

there's always a Black man in my life
a Homie found the power of spine
            percolating
with ways to
shorten
my crisis
extend   my   climax
this man is there
even when it's a drag for him
he steps through the shadows
becomes an incorruptible senator
the instant my troubling light
falls on his empathetic face
& right away
he's gathering all the facts
gaveling
to start a public hearing
with hours as convenient as a 7-11

there's always a Black man who grants my wishes
a Walkboy lined his pockets with psalms
            ripening
with ways to
soothe
my doubt
prolong   my   high
that man is here
even when confusion weakens his meaning
he steps through the contradictions
becomes a medicating genie
soon as we make eye contact
& right away
he's floating up under my confessions
X-raying through the bullshit
sifting for faults

measuring for serenity
while always
speaking his revelations
like Miles on *All Blues*

there's always a Black man in my life
my man
laughing desert water in my ears

erupting
so unstatistical
living
for more than just the weekend

24-7...
we're crammed between
every second of our lives
without a mirror's yardstick
without a hint
that any generosity
will be reimbursed
& in the grinding
steady guarding against specified meltdowns

there are Black men in our lives
always
yes, Black men
in our lives
there's always a Black man in our lives
always
in our lives
alive alive alive   *well*

AMERICAN MAN

So many of them ... on the avenue of speechlessness ...
Please come Great Voice"
– Larry Neal

militant falsetto
subtle as background radiation   indivisible as dark matter
disciplined as a second-string infielder poised to turn two in an exhibition game
umpired by prison inmates   leaping to avoid concussion of one-note meanings
barreling out of American history

whose child am I?
genuflecting to the reverb of Curtis Mayfield's mantras in 3-minute anthems?
even spreading bubble gum to repave the avenue of speechlessness
whispering the Great Voice so gentle a Christian aunt feels my love

I still get asked

how can you be an American man?
just nudging my volume past protocol frightens the uninitiated
how can you be a Black man?
just frowning in concentration intimidates Topps card collectors

> *Peter, you ain't Black. You vegetarian!*
is how Jessica put pestle into mortar after class one day
virtuoso grand daughter of the voice for integrity
converting agony of foremothers chained within clauses of declarations
flinging alchemy & medicine from tectonics of puberty
> vexing barometers of who can I be
throwing out inevitability at first base by a mile with her brash jubilation
wise-cracking adolescent   resolution in her exuberance   discerning *comadre* of
my masculine independence

CONSECRATED OFFERING

steel ripens into bird of paradise
April smelted from gifts in the periodic table
& sweat soaking a master drummer's forearms
insinuating tambourine stitches single dancers
into a circle hissing with the alchemy of unlocking shackles
shivering in the friction of transformation
        iron into sequin   slavery into jewelry
forged from bees wax   rhythm   passion
                haunting crossroads at *Ile Ife*
meaning unsheathed from metal
stunned as a cymbal consecrated by a master's sticks & splashing sweat
      reverence in paint   arch in stirred pigment
              stem of holiness at the unguarded root
of dangerous witness & committed living

sip from a woman's tilted neck
blush at her curved shoulder
bow at her foot poised between heel & toe

of what elements are dancers made?
      combustion   concussion   offering
believing hands
      ripening flower   smelting April
             finding haven in the fusion of still movement

CRITERIA

"do the doables..."
- —Wangari Maathai, Kenyan ecologist, human rights advocate,
2004 Nobel Peace Prize winner

behavior craving
scrapple of recombination
to the e c h o of Big Bang
a good taste
e x p a n d i n g mouths of fellow citizens
for billions of years

subatomic hallelujah extrapolated from Aunt Anna's merciless apple cobbler
dinner invitation contains countdown to rural Virginia queries
from master teacher prodding city-boy apprentice

whose eyes appraise mastery? bear invisible gift of correlating guidance
whose words harbor tenderness? blast along oscillating Ring Shout

do the doables say my border-melting *tias*
baby-sit the ephemeral   know the truth of a tree
coax vision into a voice   traffic in music feelings gave you back in the day
cornrow a kora's poignancy into aurora of an evening horizon
disarm overseers denouncing our song as a crime
shoo shadows from the threshold of wisdom
play bid whist with the ghost of my mother
Hula-hoop across Golden Gate Bridge   chant names of rivet slingers who fell
into churning ocean during construction
tap meanings between facts to embroider our tools
guarantee just enough structure to shoulder human virtuosity

come on in   less shock and way more awe   way more mending & coalescing into
stark raving sane   hinged & swinging without squeak of military cadence & self
serving rationale of billionaire welfare queens foisting profit into mythology
demanding allegiances from their victims, their targets, their juries

Home Training a la mode
IRS refunds big enough to repay my 84-year-old ex-babysitter
for anchoring my parents' hard-working lives
interview Miss Joyce about reallocating the federal budget
her lullaby   her ass whippings   her common wisdom
her compassionate conservatism raw material for the sweetest topping
converting Guantanamo into a national park
where like @ Manzanar
exhibition placards run down genealogy
of the national beat-down & its ugly reverb
translated as needed to raise eyebrows & knit hands
the memory of *done*
a kiss whispering between generations

DAP

Kindness scares some people …
Don't look for hidden meanings between the lines; there are none…
— June Harris, letter to her daughter Anna, May 26, 1983

praise angled w/giving
praise subtle w/knowing

knuckles unchained
decoded through bloom of tender fist on fist
touch exquisite as empathy pressed into skin
threat without oxygen
reciprocity of ceremonial greeting

hand-drum appreciation
skin-tight antidote to lingering doubt   concentrated token
proof of mutual survival confirmed in another set of eyes
grounding amid chaos for hands drafted by war
hands hungry to intertwine fingers
exhausted from hovering over hair triggers
hands completing inclination of a mother's love
visceral safety fingerprinted w/out punishment's intonation
hands completing stories pulsing in one of my mother's rambling catch-up letters

Praise intense w/ exertion
Praise lush w/ serenade

rigorous integrity
voice disciplined as tender fist on fist
spring water invocation
churned by *cross-the-tracks* church organ
reciprocity of ceremonial living

CORDUROY GOD

corduroy god
transcendent prisoner of 7th Day exaltations   ferocious lamentations
circular interpretations promising caramel eternity   blushing above marble
clouds at divine slide from liquid collaborator to Implacable Father
demanding champagne & stoic at our sacrifice wailing prayer
listen blind baby brother   dance fool   speak laugh change
once magic carmelizes

we are haunted forever

LIFE LIFE

this season life life
this need   life life
this season
this need
this crying season
this laughing need
this peter this man this fool
need this season need this need
need this life need this foolishness

when he cry   human
when he he laugh   human
morning out the pores
night between the hands
30-year-old vinyl echoes circulate his blood
daily stamina of beauty
recreate sound beyond instinct
this moment
poised with paradox in the back pocket of his humanity
years of gratitude dancing in the near sight eyes
need this season need this need
need this life need this foolishness

REACH FOR IT

...*drop you off into some funk*....
  –*George Duke*

oh I laugh & joke but I don't play
serious as heart attacks took out Ma & daddy
daring to hula hoop while I hack the national myth
weather discomfort of being schooled in languages
emphasize gaps in my American education

> *you speak Spanish*
> *you speak Korean*
>
>> to a one-tongue city boy

> *you speak Arabic*
> *you speak Armenian*
>
>> to a black & white proverb slinger

whose last vow was in asphalt drawl
rising & clicking like Akan & Xhosa
skidding up against slur of high school junkies & hard-working alcoholics
mouth amplified by determination to hold my wisdom in congruence
with the lush reconstitution of a reason for living beyond incoherent *hateration*
daring to hone new reflexes even smack in the middle of a legislated hissy fit

> *if I reach for it*

wary of *Cointelpro* body roll & echo of narrow cast
Black Codes forbidding *my* pursuit of happiness
I will slog mud   blink away sand   wince in misunderstanding
to unearth & flip over Rosetta Stone chiseled with the key to translating our
    hippest spell
describing our most supple strategy to knit gaps in our American trepidation

inviting days & nights of timeless deliberation   playful seriousness
over documents   customs   lineage guaranteeing rights to laugh   cry   grieve   criticize
health of a people measured in fearlessness of public testimony
value of their genius measured in work of public servants

if we reach for it
eye on the prize of ending this one-note worship of veiling history
we can fandango in the rejuvenation we've conjured
respect the accent of *Ashe'* we've learned to cast
our last vow mesmerizing as swoosh of double dutch rope on asphalt
rhythmic as antidote to human violence must be if we are to rewire cultural
synapses

latitude by longitude
language by language
our last vow describing human courage as relentless   as awesome as geology
reveling while its mystery outlasts American intimidation

RISE & LISTEN

for 10 amendments & 20-11 more

listen with ears of the well-traveled healer
rise when every note in the body beckons
with kinship sifted through depths funky as 30 seconds of Larry Graham
so that the dancers just won't hide
        trampling...
subsonic as boot dance   resonant as a square mile crammed with
disciples of peoples' movements still reverberating   protecting us like charms
        trampling technicalities   stomping odious debt   stampeding legacy of
laws "for regulating Negroes and slaves in the night time"*

rise with carriage of the Fisk Jubilee soloist
listen against the grain of wannabe dynasties   counter spin every political platitude
mine the thunder in Fannie Lou Hamer's democratic grammar
you might like to hear my organ
our pose & hearing   sight & bearing
pantomiming agitators for 10 amendments & 20-11 more

getting better at my steps now   without no promenading
condemning grammar sanctifying use of child soldiers   shock & awe   IMF loan
sharks   my *winding* timed to the pulse of just how much I miss everybody right now
who cannot rise & listen without resurrecting touch of the Apocalypsonian

        born of sperm charmed as a look of love
        born of ovum perfumed as a look of love

the Apocalypsonian who visits my sleep after a day of mischief embossing my enemies
who protects my children & safeguards in a black shopping bag carbon embers
compressed from social rage unleashed after Martin's assassination
the Apocalypsonian who quiets my fears   who is my trustworthy ally
speaks with innuendo of blues couplets   calypso rhymes
who makes me feel sexy as the smell of satisfaction
daring me to rise & listen   trample & *wind*...

my hips the centrifuge spinning like the well traveled healer
reanimating kinship sifted through funky thumbing of Larry Graham

> *listen to the voices*

a medium   for democratic grammar for 10 amendments & 20-11 more

** For Regulating Negroes and Slaves in the Night Time," 1731 law by
"order of Common Council" of NY*

SING OVER ME

sing over me   *VoiceMusic* of resurrection & sorcery

I am haunted by quiet footsteps of fragile mortality
premature ascension, a leaking sensation in my mind
glimpsing homicidal gaze at my profile
losing concentration against blood-lust corroding a nation's central nervous system
radioactive history inflaming drizzle   poisoning drinking water
help me do more than stagger under thunder   shift weight of
this insistent legacy of supremacies
accelerate decay of rationales for torture & torment
infuse breath with indivisible molecules of mended bonds
I want you to sing over me
I keep forgetting my lyrics   fingering wrong notes on thumb piano at sunrise
time traveling till noonday's percussionist lapses into heartburn & arrhythmia
snatching
from midair snarling *Chitlin Circuit* notes floated by a spooked organist soloing at
sundown   scraping diamond tip across unscratched LPs of dreamtime encoded
with timeless memories   submerge me into visions mapping journeys altered by
brainwave & the shudder of hum & moan & song ...
... between us all ...
lingering ...
droning ...
... seal the deal w/some way other solo   angled away from story stuck suffocating
life-saving solvency of VoiceMusic slowly unveiling meanings like an LP after,
like, an ecstatic Soul Train dancer in 3-inch platform shoes drops into a split &
kicks plug out the socket on a DJ's counter-spinning turntables
sing to the cute, crew-cut boy squinting into the sun
cross-eyed with confusion
shy in front of camera lens   wise to the asymmetry of childhood
prisoner of a Play Mother's Home Training
sing to man thrilled being midwifed   I hear mallets cradle my day-breaking voice
sway to organ draped by silk shoulder wrap   stunned that a DJ can miraculously
mix opening bass line & voice of Marvin & Tammi's *You're All I Need (To Get By)*
with opening finger snaps & voices of *Your Precious Love* ...
s e e p Magnificence & Beauty into me ... between cracks of sidewalks where I

only want to stroll with a snack & a skip in my step   dancing to my girlfriend's
sexy chatter through earphones & to the splash of rain saturating dusk with a
round-the-way melody should make even a seasoned vampire lose all numbness
sing over me   a transfusion for decapitated verse   a homing signal   tutorial
rhythm .... I want you to lean back in joy   anger at no one when I retreat from
the seizure of hunger returning   sit me up with dancer's attitude, skin glowing
hotter than pulsing stage lights, aura fanning from my posture   repositioned by
the choreography of your song for me

THE NEXT MALCOLM POEM

the next Malcolm poem
celebrates the last midnight
a father took quiet giant steps
through the moonlit halls of his home
his whispers a bedtime flute soothing
the breath of his sleeping daughters
humming *Mona Lisa* as he tiptoes
back into their mother's arms
places his spectacles on the night stand
nestles into her drowsy eyes
brushes her cheeks as he pulls
the covers up to her open throat
kissing her mouth to pass on secrets
he learned from his dreaming girls

      the next Malcolm poem
      celebrates the first morning
      the hero's wife took healing giant steps
      onto the road past memory toward eternity
      her whispers a Coltrane soprano soloing
      up the spine of her sheltered daughters
      humming *Naima* as she weans them from grief
      floats out of widowhood
      dedicated to the ones she loves
      steels herself against fantastic
      first-name justifications
      steeps herself in the spicy occasion
      she chose life over death
      willing another set of fingerprints
      to the biographers who come to praise the name
      Shabazz

NOTHING

40 new years   schooled   scolded
by blues   love
faith of patient children
turned out between thighs & sunrise
catching me naked & unharmed
spoiled overnight
a mannish boy
risk plain on the face of a groaning man
fulfillment shimmers in droplets on my skin
evaporates before day's revelation scalds me

my waking a sensation
answer prayers I never even heard spoke
echo hymns steep between pauses when Black folk talk
my hair a prism
break my light into surprise & mystery
prove money cannot choose my mother & father
or pay rain maker to end drought
my eyes a mirror
break my sight into reflection & vision
elongate the peace of my easy acceptance

I still don't know nothing
not one thing
nothing I do   nothing I wish
promise new year
nothing I say   nothing I trust
promise new breath

a mannish boy bows out to a grown man
grateful for
love   blues
patience for faithful children
rinse my mouth with nothing better
than wonder simmered for spring vintage

read my only instructions fineprinted on this hand written label
mark the calendar of the instant
study the bible in each touch
spoil yourself in the scolding
find yourself in the schooling

VETTING MYSELF FOR HUMAN OFFICE

on a move out front of feral gossip staccato footsteps & ominous *knock knock*
through trepidation to claim sacred place where grown folk get down

a descendant of Virginia slavery my light-skinned Black mother dues I have paid
                              (& *ever wonderful in my own sweet way*)
CAT-scans distinctions between white folk & white supremacists
embraces his check-mate of *asterisked* legacy of U.S. atonality
discerns uniqueness & *same-o same-o* of cultures different than mine

finds shelter in hairy women   dreadlocked scholars   principled dissenters
stylish servants of dispossessed children rigorous sensualists determined to
pierce complacency
all 'n all lovers who swear they sway to close-eyed saxophone when I grovel in
their ear   patriots who salute the spaces between stars & stripes

remain most electrified by megahertz of *City Country City* Black folk
who holler at movie screens w/ impeccable timing
braid & tame baby girl's hair into 3 strands w/yellow red & blue barrettes
transform bid whist games into scenes mined by August Wilson
preserve tickets from Frankie Beverly & Maze concerts
forgive Marvin Gaye's father

my dead parents & extended family
my truest prism for religious behavior
my warning against fealty to round-the-way predictabilities
American consumption routines & Lord Have Mercy soliloquies

I am vetting myself for human office
renouncing allegiance to absolutes & taboos
soaking w/in contradictions & consequences
cascading co-opted standards of allure & consecration
dousing flames of witch burnings
sucking my teeth & calling out agents of inquisitions & slave raiders
cloaking my brainwaves from satellite's overpass

removing bookmarks from literature some man vows whispered to him
by a God who sanctions gang-banging as Conversion Rite

all my skeletons unchained   all my closet doors unhinged
my membership card ripped along its perforations
an orphan stealing away to find family of grown folk
defending our home against feral gossip staccato footsteps & ominous *knock knock*
of straight razors dressed in starch taking notes w/ light pens
smearing infrared ink across liquid crystal
talking out of school & into their ear pieces
threatening to spill secrets if I don't keep my mouth shut
about my flesh & blood blisters & mysteries

      Psst...

      say he African but we possess photos of him nuzzling between
a Cover Girl's legs
      say he straight but we got footage of him open arms on a Unity
Fellowship Sunday
      say he respect women but we bugged his shouts to staged sex of
dot cum websites
      say he ecological but Map Quest download his gas-guzzling routes
into taxpayer wilderness
      say he patriotic but he won't masturbate to our manufactured innocence
      say he your friend but when's last time he had you over for a
home-cooked meal & leisurely celebration

      watch him   don't trust him   censor him

check for Styrofoam in his recycle bin
swipe his cell phone signals
swab his DNA
burn down the firewall on his Macintosh
subpoena his library records
interrogate owners of independent bookstores
dub his music collection
watch who come to his parties

he will break   he will conform
bid him in   bid him in

here's my business card

call me if he acts like a man who's stripped off his bar code
call me if he acts like a man who believes he is free

COMPLETE ALREADY

no more hoarding loveliness

giving dap to hummingbird w/a gold tooth

no more

singing back-up to mountain creek song

ooh baby baby

complete already in me
faith when mortality creep make me more vulnerable than smokey
buckle my knees in gratitude when I taste luscious first kiss
of next morning after a day of 9-5 mediocrity
complete already in me

more loveliness where that come from

sadness is a chemical

one atom away from joy
heroism is a spiritual
one history away from slavery

day before my death

I'm throwing a going-away barbecue
for a hummingbird w/ a gold tooth who bring a dragonfly to the GoGo
blending mountain creek song
w/tomatoes onions & miracles for my special sauce
analyzing my last will & testament
w/ CPA firm of blue jay owl & crane
mailing translation of each of daddy's proverbs
in a chain letter written in ink made from
crushed cowrie shells & pomegranate seeds
phasing into *Temptations* sheen got lesbians dreaming about my fine ass
webcasting sound of my last orgasm on *myspace*

day of my death

pour me head first into our water table
one more acre foot to quench my grandson's thirst
open your mouth & reflect light off your gold voice box
grieve simply

knowing already in you
body don't speak nonsense
meditate on how many books you've eaten
        how many hamburgers you've read
dress your future in guilt-free blue suit
instruct choir director to rev up Hip Hop Hymns
about healthy visions in hello eyes of possibility
dictate my obituary without rehearsal
print it on a recycled sheet of emergence

                        stop hoarding your loveliness
I have jumped off the cliff

                                stop

cliff has caught me

                      complete already in you
I never hit the ground
          making waves sacrificed in still purity

every distance between us collapsed
intimacy incessant
select atom you need to transform sadness into joy
peel off memory w/ enough nourishment to keep mediocrity at bay
harmonize w/ song of my final orgasm
stir me into your already

                day after my death
shout
he tried
relapsed every now & then under pressure of getting with it
but he bopped
face chapped from rubbing up against his weakness
until he heard backbeat of an anthem bobbing inside him again
tell somebody
investigate his nooks & cranky
see if you ain't ambushed by a sense of humor
a tall tale

                  sweat of a nigger reconsidering

yeast of a brother w/his head to the sky
                    song of a man reconstructing
                                     say hey of a human living novocaine free

ooh baby baby already in him
hope already *hit it & quit it*
already washed by knowing
in a minute leaking from every action
already filling every pore

Acknowledgments

Grateful acknowledgment is made to the editors of the following publications in which these poems or earlier versions of them previously appeared:

The Juice Bar, by L.K. Thayer, on-line magazine, Los Angeles (2012) –
"Corduroy God"
www.lkthayer.wordpress.com/2012/12/12/curduroy-god-by-peter-j-harris/

Brooklyn & Boyle, Art & Life in Boyle Heights and Beyond, (2009) –
"Water Is Wide"

Intensidad, an art/poetry exhition, (2009) –
"Grooved Pavement Ahead" (excerpt)

Speechless the Magazine, (Winter/Spring 2005) –
 "The Lost Song of Donny Hathaway"

Random Agenda, (2005, Number 1) –
"Reach for It," "Rift Valley Girl"

Beyond the Frontier, (2002, Black Classic Press),
edited by E. Ethelbert Miller –
"I Know I Ain't Hip No More," "The Next Malcolm Poem"

Rivendell, (Winter 2002, Volume 1, Number 1) – "Bless the Ashes,"
"Night Around My Sleep "

Tenderheaded: A Comb-Bending Collection of Hair Stories,
edited by Juliette Harris & Pamela Johnson (2001) –
"Don't Even Pretend (The Saturn Poem)"

The Ethiops Ear, Claremont, CA (2000) –
"First Thing Out My Mouth"

The Global Citizen, textbook for first-year students at Chapman College,
Orange, CA (1998) –
"The Ocean Is Ours"

360 Degrees: A Revolution of Black Poets,
edited by Kalamu ya Salaam w/ Kwame Alexander (1998) –
"A Sense of Ceremony"

The Bridge Magazine, Washington, D.C. (1997) –
"Horn Section"

Prophetic Voices Magazine, Claremont, CA (1997) –
"Cult Leader in Training"

Image Magazine, Los Angeles (1995) –
"There's Always a Black Man"

Catalyst, Atlanta (1994) –
"A Sense of Ceremony"

Ramsess Jazz Calendar,
edited by Jocelyn Stewart, Los Angeles (1993) –
"There's Always a Black Man"

The Black Scholar (1996) –
"The Ocean Is Ours"

Greenfield Review, Greenfield, NY (1982) –
"From Washington Post/Nov. 13, 1980"

Goblets, Wilmington, DE (1982) –
"Delighted He Could Play God"

About the Author

PETER J. HARRIS, founder and Artistic Director of Inspiration House, has since the 1970s published his poetry, essays, and fiction in a wide range of national publications; worked as a publisher, journalist, editor and broadcaster; and been an educator and workshop leader for adults and adolescents. Harris is also founding director of The Black Man of Happiness Project, a creative, intellectual and artistic exploration of Black men and joy: www.blackmanofhappiness.com

He's author of the *The Black Man of Happiness: In Pursuit of My 'Inalienable Right,'* a book of personal essays. www.blackmanofhappiness.com/shop.

With his brother Glenn Harris, Emmy-winning broadcaster and humanitarian in Washington, D.C., Harris co-wrote *Gritt Tuff Play Book: Hard Core Wisdom for Young People,* the inaugural publication of the Happiness Project.

He's author of the joyful book, *The Vampire Who Drinks Gospel Music: The Stories of Sacred Flow & Sacred Song,* which takes readers from darkened movie houses filled with enthusiastic narrators, to the Washington, D.C., campus of Howard University, to covens illuminated by masterful art and hidden in plain sight off the coast of Georgia and outside *Ile Ife* in West Africa: [www.lulu.com/shop/peter-j-harris/the-vampire-who-drinks-gospel-music-the-stories-of-sacred-flow-and-sacred-song]

In 2011, he was a Contributor-Collaborator with his daughter Adenike Harris on her Creative Thesis: *Restorative Notions: Regaining My Voice, Regaining My Father: A Creative Womanist Approach to Healing from Sexual Abuse,* Georgia State University [www.digitalarchive.gsu.edu/wsi_theses/23], a candid, ethical, loving dialogue between a Black father and a Black daughter confronting, surviving, and transcending her rape by a Black step father.

Harris co-edited *Relive Everything & Live the Same: VoiceMusic from Avenue 50's Black-Brown Dialogues Project,* an anthology published by Avenue 50 Studio, Los Angeles (2011). He wrote the forward to *New Wine and Black Men's Feet* by Keith Antar Mason (2010, Red Hen Press). His essay, "1,000 O'clock: Johnson Time," was published in the 2009 anthology, *The Black Body,* edited by Meri Danquah (Seven Stories Press). Harris is author of *The Johnson Chronicles: Truth & Tall Tales about My Penis* and *Safe Arms: 20 Love/Erotic Poems (and One Ooh Baby Baby Moan).* His magazine, *Genetic Dancers: The Artistry Within African/American Fathers,* published during the 1980s, was the first magazine of its kind and asserted that African American fathers become artists through the frictions of conscientious parenting.

His book *Hand Me My Griot Clothes: The Autobiography of Junior Baby*, featured a philosophical elder Black man ruminating on life, love, and ethics, and won the PEN Oakland award for multicultural literature in 1993. His personal essays about manhood and masculinity have been published in several anthologies, including *Tenderheaded: A Comb-Bending Collection of Hair Stories; Black Men Speaking; Fathersongs; I Hear a Symphony: African Americans Celebrate Love;* and *What Makes a Man: Twenty-two Writers Imagine the Future.*